CLASSIC
QUILTS

CLASSIC
QUILTS

Ruth McKendry

Photographs by Blake McKendry

Patterns by Lucy Anne Holliday

KEY PORTER BOOKS

Canadian Cataloguing in Publication Data

McKendry, Ruth, 1920–
    Classic quilts

ISBN 1-55013-775-1

1. Bedding – Ontario – History – 19th century. 2. Quilts – Ontario – History – 19th century. 3. Quilting – Ontario – History – 19th century. 4. Frontier and pioneer life – Ontario. I. Title.

NK9113.A3065   1997   746.9'7'0971309034   C97-930498-6

Key Porter Books Limited
70 The Esplanade
Toronto, Ontario
Canada M5E 1R2

Design: Leah Gryfe

Distributed in the United States by Firefly Books

Printed and bound in Spain

97 98 99 00 6 5 4 3 2 1

For reasons of space, the following abbreviations have been used in the text.
C.C.F.C.S.: Canadian Centre for Folk Culture Studies, National Museum
    of Civilization, Ottawa, Ontario.
S.S.M.: Scugog Shores Museum, Port Perry, Ontario.
P.C.: private collection.

Page 2: Friendship Sampler Quilt: appliquéd; cotton and polyester; made by Kingston Heirloom Quilters, 1982. W. 256 cm, L. 213 cm (101, 84 in.). Each block was sewn by the person who signed it. Handsome tulip swag and small sawtooth border lighten and unite the overall design.

Contents

Preface..7

CHAPTER 1
Fruit of Her Hands................................11

CHAPTER 2
The Quilting Bee and the Marriage Bed.................43

CHAPTER 3
The Quilt Makers................................51

CHAPTER 4
Quilt Patterns, Their Meanings and Origins.................59

CHAPTER 5
Quilts of the Pioneers................................89

General Instructions, or Helpful Hints.................98

Endnotes................................116

Bibliography................................116

Index................................118

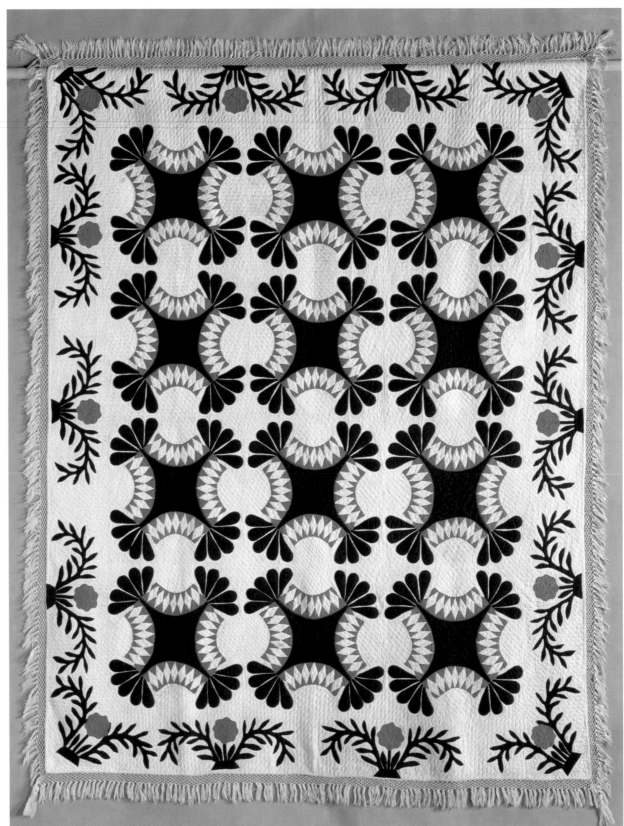

Preface

OVER THE YEARS, I HAVE LOOKED AT MANY QUILTS and talked to quilt makers in Canada and the United States, and I have been fascinated by the fact that I have rarely seen two identical quilts, although the same standard patterns were used again and again. The differences then must lie in the minds and attitudes of those who did the work. This realization reinforced my feeling that a woman's personality is mirrored in her quilts.

As a woman sits at home alone in the afternoon, working on a quilt, the changing passions and seasons of her life are reflected forever in her stitches. Into her quilts she works her dreams and fears and hopes. A young woman making her marriage quilt sews red roses to express the passion she feels for the man with whom she will one day share her bedcover. A weeping willow stitched by an old woman into her bedcover is a memory of a love lost years ago but never forgotten. Some women with their needles invoke the good spirits, and with ancient symbols frighten away the evil ones. A country woman safeguards a loved one by repeatedly piecing the initials H–L, for Holy Lord, into the pattern of her quilt. Like me, many older women, during their childhood, slept warm and safe in frigid bedrooms beneath quilts made by mothers and grandmothers. Love went into the making of those quilts, and it was a comforting feeling to sleep under quilts made by kind and familiar hands. The good spirits invoked by love and devotion safeguarded us from the dark and evil demons of the night. A baby wrapped in the folds of a cradle quilt, made with love and faith, is as safe as in the womb. An aging grandmother makes an Old Brown Goose quilt for a beloved grandchild, hoping the lullaby she sings for him will comfort him in the terrors of the night.

OPPOSITE PAGE: *Whig's Defeat (variant): quilt, appliquéd; quilting outline, crosshatch; cotton; made by Jessie Campbell, Huntingdon, Quebec, ca. 1860. W. 222.5 cm, L. 175.1 cm (87, 69 in.). Agnes Etherington Art Centre, Queen's University. Gift of Ross and Katherine Anderson, 1989.*

*Beaver: quilt,
appliquéd; cotton;
machine-quilted;
Quebec, ca. 1920.
Beavers, baskets,
branches, and clusters
of acorns; sawtooth
border. [P.C.]*
✿

Sometimes I pause to marvel at the glorious quilts that emerged from modest little houses with no central heating, no electricity, and no plumbing. Yet quilts are perishable items with which to mark one's immortality. My great-aunt Maggie Dewar made at least three quilts every winter in the little clapboard-covered log house where she lived. She gave them as presents to sisters and nieces, grandnieces and cousins. Ten years after her death, of all those quilts, I was able to locate only two—a third one had been cut down for a crib from a worn double. At first this appalled me, but then I began to wonder if perhaps the true role of a quilt is its function as a bedcover that warms and blesses those who sleep under it. Perhaps it is enough that, day after day, a young bride gazed with admiration at the pleasing symmetry of the simple pattern and felt comforted by the gentle harmony of its colors. And perhaps the carefully wrought fertility symbols Auntie placed on all bridal quilts were in part responsible for further additions to her family of great-great-nieces and nephews. Goodness knows how many children were conceived under (and occasionally on top of) Auntie's bridal quilts!

Every spring the quilts Auntie had given over the years to her young relatives waved from clotheslines in towns and cities in the East and the West, across Canada and the United States, and passersby in all those places shared their gentle messages. Not a single quilt spent its days and nights folded in a musty-smelling blanket chest or trunk. If the virtue of an everyday object lies in its function, then Auntie's quilts received their true measure of esteem.

I am interested in writing about the women who made quilts, women whose household chores revolved around the more important hours they spent making quilts, women who skipped lunch because they would rather quilt than eat, farm women who had to fit their quilt making into the seasons when the harvest was over and before the plowing and seeding began, women who captured the ethereal flight of the swallow with a few bits of leftover cloth, and a woman who worked a falling star into her quilt to keep in mind forever a lost, unborn child.

Fruit of Her Hands

She seeketh wool, and flax, and worketh willingly
with her hands…
She layeth her hand to the spindle, and her hands
hold the distaff…
Give her of the fruit of her hands; and let her own works
praise her in the gates.

—Proverbs 31: 13–31

FROM ANCIENT TIMES IN EUROPE AND ASIA, WOMEN have created warmth and strength in bedclothing by quilting, or sewing together two layers of cloth with a filling in between. Very little of this early quilting remains. However, the few remnants that have survived indicate that these were not primitive efforts, but that fine needlework was used in the process. Even in later times, the quilting of bedcovers was woman's work, and it was enjoyed as one of the few art forms available in the restricted world of the female. Men, other than certain tradesmen who were sometimes employed to mark or trace an elaborate design on an article that was to be quilted, had no part in this exclusive field.

When a woman made a quilt, her ever-changing moods and the different stages of her life were often reflected in it. In early times her attitudes were expressed symbolically and with considerable restraint, but as time went by, these expressions became less constrained, although still formal. Symbolic motifs became more overt, and eventually they evolved into easily interpreted representations of ideas. Modern quilt makers make little attempt to hide their feelings and moods, and even when a woman attempts to do so, an involuntary reflection of her state of mind can often be found in her creation. In the late twentieth century men,

OPPOSITE PAGE:
Hovering Hawks:
quilt, pieced; cotton;
small patterned reds,
blues, and white;
Leeds County,
Ontario, 1st quarter
20th century. W. 152
cm, L. 187 cm (60, 74
in.). There is one red
triangle in the center
of each block, a device
that effectively lightens
and unites the pattern.
[C.C.F.C.S.]

too, occasionally make quilts to express their artistic talents.

A quilt, as I've said, consists of two layers of cloth with some soft substance between. To keep the three layers from shifting, they are tacked together in some manner. They may be tied with short pieces of yarn, or sewn (quilted) together, usually in a pattern, by running stitches through the layers. In general there are two types of quilts: wholecloth and patchwork. When the top layer of the quilt is made from a single piece of cloth (which may be seamed to achieve the desired width), the bedcovering is called a wholecloth quilt (p. 13). In this quilt, the stripes in the pattern are woven into the cloth. In most Canadian quilts, the top layer consists of several small pieces or patches of cloth. These are known as patchwork quilts. They, too, are divided into two types: pieced, as in Hovering Hawks (p. 10), and appliquéd, as in Old Rose of Sharon (p. 14). The top of the pieced patchwork consists of many small pieces of cloth seamed together in a manner that may or may not form a pattern, while in the appliquéd version, small pieces of cloth are sewn onto a single piece of foundation cloth to form a pattern. Both types of patchwork quilts may be made with all-over designs, or they may be made in units, called blocks, which are then seamed together to form a whole.

To set means to put the quilt together; the *set* refers to the strips or squares of cloth joining the pieced or appliquéd blocks. Alternatively, the blocks can be sewn together edge to edge as in all-over quilt patterns. In the case of all-over appliquéd quilts, the pattern patches are sewn to foundation cloth that is the size of the finished quilt. Because extra fabric is needed to lay the pattern pieces over the foundation or ground cloth—instead of seaming the patches together edge to edge—appliquéd bedcovers were considered more prestigious when cloth was scarce. In the United States and Canada, the lively and colorful patchwork quilt, either pieced or appliquéd, was more popular than the wholecloth variety. The complications of sewing the many patterns together to achieve the desired effect are so varied that it is evident that most quilt makers visualized the completed quilt as a picture.

Although the making of quilts was an important domestic industry in the Old World, it assumed even greater importance in the New World, where warm bedding was essential in the surprisingly cold climate. In the years before 1860 or so, quilts made in Canada reflected the ethnic origins of the people who made them. There were two main influences:

Wholecloth Quilt: homewoven from handspun wool; orange and gray stripes; Renfrew County, Ontario, 4th quarter 19th century. W. 170 cm, L. 177 cm (67, 70 in.). Quilted in sweeping curves to form a large diamond in the center. The back is made from homewoven, handspun wool, and the filling is loose wool. The entire quilt is quilted with homespun yarn, a tremendous undertaking. [P.C.]

Old Rose of Sharon or Rose Cross: quilt, appliquéd; cotton; Napanee, Ontario, ca. 1859. W. 162 cm, L. 208 cm (64, 82 in.). A beautifully made quilt with very fine quilting. [P.C.]

✡

European and American. Immigrants from England, Ireland, Scotland, France, and some Central European countries brought their own styles, ones that had not changed much during the previous century. Around the same time, settlers of various ethnic origins from the United States brought with them the distinctive styles that had been developing in that country during the hundred years or so of settlement.

Nevertheless, conditions in the new land of Canada were unique, and quilts reflected this difference. The making of bedding in the old, settled lands, where there was always a backlog of bedding and cloth within a family, was a leisurely affair. More urgency existed in this cold, lonely country, where there was little or no cloth and where there were few relatives to help make new bedding.

France did not have a strong tradition of quilt making, and there is little evidence that the first French settlers in Lower Canada made many quilts. Early on, women in Quebec established the tradition of making woven bedding. Inventories taken around the beginning of the eighteenth century describe imported bedcovers in rich houses, while in poorer homes people used feather mattresses covered with deerskin, moose skins, buffalo robes, and woven bedspreads. In the same inventories there is mention of only one small English quilt and one of homespun drugget.[1]

By the last quarter of the eighteenth century, quilts were apparently being used. A German officer traveling in 1776 wrote: "As soon as you are out of bed it is made up and covered with a quilt of silesia, calico, or wool with the ends hanging down over the sides. The poorest inhabitant has such a covering for his bed …"[2] This was doubtless a whole-cloth quilt, made of either imported woolen cloth (silesia) or, in poorer homes, of homewoven cloth made from homespun wool. There is little evidence of this style of quilt in Quebec today, although a few patchwork wool quilts such as Geometric Star (p. 16) have survived.

During the nineteenth and twentieth centuries, Quebec women became interested in quilt making. An elderly man told me his mother was a quilt maker, but the instructions for the patterns she used were in English; he remembered because sometimes she asked him to translate. Quilts made in Quebec can often be identified by the fine, closely spaced rows of quilting (p. 16); a small hanging diamond or lozenge pattern was favored. The quilts made by women in Glengarry County in Ontario, which borders on Quebec, share a distinctive style with those

ABOVE: *Geometric Star: quilt, pieced; wool, some homespun patches; orange-red with blacks and grays; made by Annie McGregor, Soulanges County, Quebec, 3rd quarter 19th century. W. 163 cm, L. 167 cm (64, 66 in.). Color is used sparsely but effectively.* [P.C.]

✪

RIGHT: *Birds in a Tree: quilt, appliquéd; cotton; red, green, and white; Quebec, 3rd quarter 19th century. W. 172 cm, L. 182 cm (68, 72 in.). This is an unusual design—birds, trees, and stars, with a hammock border. The central tree has a hole in which an object, possibly a nest, can be seen. The quilting lines are so close together that they ripple.* [C.C.F.C.S]

✪

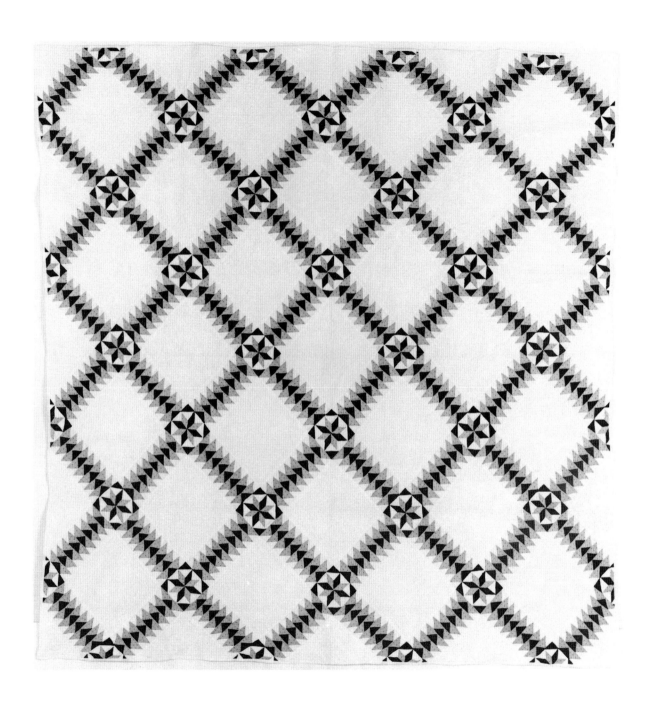

Double Wild Goose Chase and Star: quilt, pieced; cotton; white and red; made by Mme Harpin, St. Ours, Quebec, ca. 1900. W. 202 cm, L. 202 cm (79, 79 in.). Quilted in the fine hanging diamond pattern favored by Quebec quilters. [P.C.]

✧

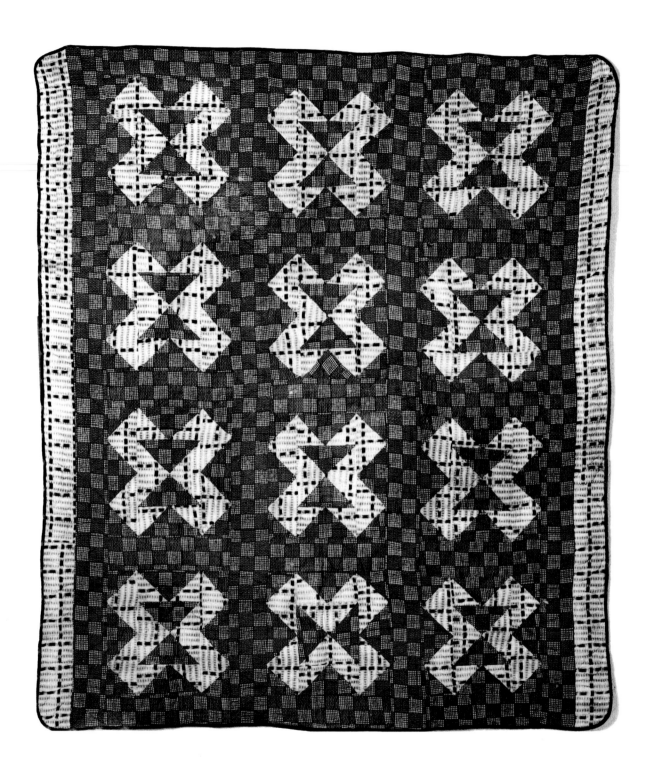

Old Brown Goose: quilt, pieced; cotton; made by Elizabeth Hannah McAndrew,
Newboyne, Saskatchewan, 4th quarter 19th century. W. 173 cm, L. 197 cm (68, 77 in.).
Although this pattern gets its name from the lullaby "The Old Gray Goose," it was usually
made in brown, a more pleasing color for bedding. [C.C.F.C.S]

✿

made by women in Quebec. The Double Wild Goose Chase and Star (p. 17) made in Quebec is almost identical to one made in Glengarry, even to the quilting design. One seldom-seen pattern called the French Star is said to be completely Canadian in origin; it does not appear in the United States, but it is difficult to say where it originated. A French Star quilt was made by Elizabeth Fennel Van Alstine (1831–1894) in Napanee, Ontario; her family came from Ireland. The popular Lemon Star is thought to have originally been Les Moines Star.

Quilt patterns are similar in Ontario and the Maritime provinces, although pattern names differ. Hole in the Barn Door, for example, is called Fisherman's Reel in the Maritimes. Fewer early quilts of handwoven woolen cloth have survived in the Maritime provinces than in Ontario, where a considerable number of early woolen quilts can still be found. Like the women of Quebec, Maritime women liked colorful, handwoven, homespun blankets and handwoven woolen coverlets. The cloth from some of their warm quilts may have been converted into the rag rugs that were so popular in the Maritimes. The women in the eastern provinces took pride in their handiwork, and they made many good quilts in the late nineteenth and early twentieth centuries using the patterns fashionable at the time.

Generally speaking, certain patterns were fashionable throughout the country during certain years. Because of late settlement, quilts sewn in the western provinces were made at a period when designs were chosen almost entirely from American pattern books and Canadian newspapers. Some quilts traveled out west with people who moved there from the rest of Canada. The settlers from Ontario in the last quarter of the nineteenth century and the first quarter of the twentieth century tended to take with them their newer quilts. Elizabeth Hannah McAndrew, born in Newboyne, Saskatchewan, in the middle of the nineteenth century, made several interesting quilts, which were kept by members of her family. The patterns Old Brown Goose (p. 18), Chimney Sweep (p. 20), and different versions of Delectable Mountains (p. 21, p. 23, p. 25) are familiar ones, but the wide variety of colorful fabrics in the quilts suggest that the quilt maker was able to choose from many materials on the store shelves of her father who was a store keeper and fur trader.

While Central European settlers in the western provinces preferred to make colorful, handwoven bedcovers in their own distinctive styles,

Chimney Sweep: quilt, pieced; cotton, filled with dark-red wool (buffalo?); brown cotton prints on white with brown stripes; made by Elizabeth Hannah McAndrew, Newboyne, Saskatchewan, 4th quarter 19th century. W. 147 cm, L. 188 cm (58, 74 in.). The brown and white designs make an attractive blend. [C.C.F.C.S]

✧

Delectable Mountains: quilt, pieced, square-in-square format; cotton; rosy red and blue on a white background; made by Elizabeth Hannah McAndrew, Newboyne, Saskatchewan, 4th quarter 19th century. W. 170 cm, L. 175 cm (67, 69 in.). [C.C.F.C.S]

✿

rather than quilts, during the late nineteenth and early twentieth centuries, women of other ethnic origins, in Manitoba, Saskatchewan, Alberta, and British Columbia, made quilts similar to those made in the rest of Canada. At the present time in those provinces, enthusiastic quilting guilds meet and sew colorful, imaginative interpretations of the usual patterns, and quilt exhibitions continue to stimulate interest everywhere.

British Columbia has some very enthusiastic quilters, and both traditional and art quilts are being made there. The Canadian Quilt Study Group originated in that province and has a wide membership throughout Canada and the United States. Such organizations stoke the fires of creativity among quilt makers, who are eager to learn more about a favorite activity. Now that quilting has become an artistic endeavor rather than a domestic necessity, whether one makes a quilt to hang on a wall or put on a bed is a matter of individual preference. The aesthetic quality of the product is a serious issue, but most important of all is the pleasure people derive in creativity.

Ontario has a good selection of early quilts. One reason is simply that Ontario had a large population. Also, the early settlers and their descendants were cautious, thrifty people who tended to remain in the original homesteads and did not lightly part with family heirlooms. Ontario has a wealth of early patchwork quilts made of handwoven, homespun wool. The style probably arrived from Scotland with the earliest settlers, and flourished in this province.

All immigrant women coming into Canada brought with them the customs of their home countries, regardless of the date of their arrival. But from the earliest years, the art of quilt making, especially of patchwork quilts, took on a new life in the adopted country because of the cold climate and different lifestyle. Most early immigrants were young or middle-aged, since the elderly or infirm were usually unable to undertake the difficult journey across the ocean and through the forests. Neighbors were scarce, and homesteads were often far apart. There were few villages, and it was not easy to make the lengthy trip to a store or church. As a result, members of the community had to assist one another in major undertakings. This type of gathering was called a bee, and after the work was done there was always a party, which was frequently a rowdy affair, especially when the bee involved hard physical labor such as a barn raising.

In Canada, a young woman was expected to have ready for her

Delectable Mountains: quilt, pieced; printed cottons; reds, greens, and browns; made by Elizabeth Hannah McAndrew, Newboyne, Saskatchewan, 4th quarter 19th century. W. 157 cm, L. 180 cm (62, 71 in.). This pattern, which derives its name from Bunyan's Pilgrim's Progress, *was a favorite with 19th-century quilt makers.* [C.C.F.C.S.]

✧

marriage twelve everyday quilts, which she had begun to make when she was quite young. Sometimes she would sew the tops only; the rest was finished and quilted when she became engaged. At this time she made a special quilt, usually an appliquéd one, intended for use on her marriage bed. When the need arose to quilt several tops for a wedding, a bee would be held. In one day many hands would quilt several bed-covers for use in a bride's new home. At a bee, the women and girls were more interested in getting the job done than in counting the number of stitches to an inch. As a result, not all nineteenth-century quilts are finely or evenly quilted. Fancy designs and fine stitching were reserved for quilts made for special occasions such as weddings.

As early as the first half of the nineteenth century, some young women, such as Mary Morris (pp. 26–27) and Frances Mulligan (p. 30), both living in rural Ontario, were making beautiful wedding quilts. Those two fine examples have survived the years.

In rural areas, where most people lived in the early nineteenth century, quilting helped women overcome their loneliness. Quilt patterns, even scraps of cloth, were exchanged. The making of quilts created an agreeable bond among the women of a community, and the art of quilting took on a new vivacity in Canada, as it had in the United States.

Some of our finest quilts were made in the last half of the nineteenth century, when both the quality of style and workmanship peaked. Geometric quilts in lively, intricate patterns were designed for everyday use, and beautiful appliquéd quilts were created with loving care for special occasions. Red-and-white quilts were fashionable at this time, especially in the last quarter of the century, when a color-fast red dye became available (p. 31). Serious quilt makers still adhered rigidly to old traditions in their creations. A woman's reputation as quilt maker meant much to her. Top quilt makers in the city and the country strove to outdo one another, while those in the lower ranks cheerfully accepted their inferior place in the hierarchy and were filled with admiration for the elite.

In 1898, a catalog—then in the ninth revised edition—put out by the Ladies Art Company, St. Louis, Missouri, had more than 200 quilt patterns for sale.[3] A few years later, the same company sold cut, ready-to-sew quilt tops, which could be hand quilted for a price.[4] In 1928, they offered patterns, cut blocks, finished blocks, and hand quilting by one woman at $12.00 to $18.00, depending on the pattern. Edges finished with scal-

Delectable Mountains: quilt, pieced; cotton; light brown on deep yellow; made by Elizabeth Hannah McAndrew, Newboyne, Saskatchewan, 4th quarter 19th century. W. 202 cm, L. 165 cm (79, 65 in.). This is an unusual all-over variation of the pattern, not unlike Indian Hatchet. [P.C.]

✴

lops were $2.00 extra, with points $1.50 extra, material not provided. In addition they would make complete quilts in any colors from any design in the book. Prices ranged from $25.00 to $45.00.[5] The presence of these American catalogs in many Canadian households leads one to suspect there was considerable demand for their products. The origin of these quilts was likely a dark secret, unknown to anyone but the postmaster,

Mary Morris Quilt: multicolored, embroidered motifs on a white central medallion, with running horses, dogs, and symbols such as peacocks, swastikas, etc., on a second white border or frame; several printed cotton borders or frames; made by Mary Morris (at the age of fourteen), Elgin area, Leeds County, Ontario, 1825. W. 185 cm, L. 200 cm (73, 79 in.). Mary Morris was born in 1811 with a physical handicap that prevented her from walking. As a result, she became a skilled needlewoman at an early age. This quilt was preserved by her relatives. It is backed with handspun linen, contains little or no stuffing, and is finely quilted. [C.C.F.C.S.]

✿

Mary Morris Quilt detail, showing central medallion with flowering branch, flowers, foliage, etc. Probably all have been used symbolically.

✿

and is perhaps indicative of the status of quilt making at the time.

By the turn of the century fine quilts were still being made, but the art of quilting did not entirely escape the general deterioration in taste sometimes characteristic of the late-Victorian and early-Edwardian era. Crazy quilts, intended for parlor throws, were made of impractical velvets and silks, and usually heavily embroidered in every kind of stitch known to woman. Almost by accident, these sometimes resulted in glorious conglomerations of shapes and colors. They became an engrossing fad, and a young woman sometimes spent many hours, in this more leisurely era, searching the rag bags of her friends and neighbors for a scrap of fabric just the right color and texture to juxtapose with scraps already selected. Embroidered Scottish maidens in kilts and small boys with fishing poles abound in these quilts; a few unique items of significance to the maker are also included. An unusual and attractive crazy quilt was made by a woman in Sharbot Lake, Ontario. It includes designs of the deer and fish that flourish in that wooded area (p. 31). In Glengarry, Ontario, friends of a young woman named Hatty Fraser made her a crazy quilt generously ornamented with individual hats, each one embroidered by a friend.

These whimsical quilts were great fun to sew and served to keep younger women interested in quilt making. In this era, quilting was still a necessary part of daily life, since people were reluctant to part with their scarce supplies of cash for items they could make for much less. Blankets were expensive, and bedding was made at home more often than bought at the store.

Although it was seldom done, changing the designs in appliquéd quilts was possible. The standard patterns of pieced quilts did not easily lend themselves to variations; however, the quilt makers allowed their creative instincts to run riot with the glorious assortment of colors the rag bag provided. A venturesome quilt maker sometimes filled the rigid boundaries of a standard pattern with masses of color, much in the same way that colorful assortments of flowers sometimes overrun a formal garden.

By the beginning of the twentieth century, some women began to make quilts using more individual designs. People had slightly more money and felt freer to buy cloth. If symbols were employed, they were thought of merely as pleasing patterns. In more prosperous times, only the very old felt a need for protection from the spirits.

In many households, people were beginning to think of quilts as ornamental top covers on the bed. By the 1920s, patterns reveal a new naturalistic approach, as seen in the Apple Orchard quilt (p. 34), which portrays an orchard. Earlier tree patterns were stylized, being formed entirely from triangles, with a rectangle for the tree trunk. Tree of Paradise (p. 33) is an example: here the trees were designed as significant symbols rather than portraits. Softer colors began to appear. This may have been the result of the coming of electric lights, which made the vivid colors of the previous century look somewhat garish.

Although a number of women and a few dedicated church groups continued to quilt because the work satisfied their creative instincts, there was no doubt that enthusiasm for making quilts and the joyful excitement of the early years had begun to fade now that it was no longer essential work. Some women, unwilling to forsake quilting, made fussy, pretty quilts in pastel shades in an attempt to imitate fashionable, store-bought bedspreads.

Pattern books of the 1920s and 1930s illustrated realistic floral patterns. Gone was the stylized Jack in the Pulpit (p. 37), and in its place was the more naturalistic Three Tulips in a Pot (p. 38). While the old pieced patterns were so nonrepresentative that one could scarcely identify the pattern name, the floral patterns of the twenties and thirties looked like the flowers they portrayed, which pleased some quilt makers. Others, more traditional, felt that a quilt should communicate a feeling, or indicate a subtle message, and not just be a picture.

In order to stimulate enthusiasm for the waning art of quilt making, pattern books of the twenties and thirties boasted of several newly designed modern patterns. Sometimes these turned out to be old favorites sprouting new names. Friendship Aster became Dresden Plate. Modern patterns such as the weak and fussy Colonial Girl and Rambler Rose appeared in catalogs. Sunbonnet Sue, Overall Bill, and similar "cute" patterns were touted, and proved to be quite popular. Women liked to keep up-to-date, and made fashionable quilts, especially for the spare-room bed, which continued to be the showplace for a new acquisition. Most people made only appliquéd designs, now that imported cotton prints were cheap and readily available. In addition, the message of the quilt was no longer serious.

A few elderly women continued to cut out elaborate pieced patterns like Double Wedding Ring, which are difficult to assemble, and found

ABOVE: *Frances Mulligan Quilt: central medallion type; wool and cotton; Hazeldean area, Ontario, 1856. W. 177 cm, L. 187 cm (70, 74 in.). Frances Mulligan made this quilt at the age of sixteen. She used motifs associated with a marriage quilt: hearts, a flowering bush, etc. She died at an early age.*
[C.C.F.C.S.]

✪

RIGHT: *Frances Mulligan Quilt detail, showing scalloped circle representing female. The flowering branch, peacocks, and butterflies symbolize the renewal of life, immortality, and resurrection, respectively.*

✪

ABOVE: *Double Hearts and other motifs: quilt, appliquéd; cotton; red and white; made by Catherine McGinn, Montreal, Quebec, ca. 1865. W. 183 cm, L. 203 cm (72, 80 in.). The fabric is folded and cut along the outlines of a paper template. The pieces were applied using herringbone stitch. Agnes Etherington Art Centre, Queen's University.*

RIGHT: *Crazy: quilt, pieced; cotton and woolens; assorted bright colors; Sharbot Lake, Ontario, ca. 1930. W. 157 cm, L. 203 cm (62, 80 in.). Designs of the fish, deer, and birds that abound in this wooded area are incorporated in this charming quilt.* [C.C.F.C.S.]

that they no longer remembered how to put the pieces together and there was no one left to consult. Sometimes these colorful cut blocks turn up at auctions. People buy them now with interest, but they seldom become quilts. The day of the colorful everyday pieced quilt was over, although frugal people who sewed clothing continued to use leftover scraps, especially in children's quilts. The time had not yet arrived when most people were willing to waste cloth, although it would. After the Second World War overabundance was thought to be indicative of the good life.

A young woman in the 1920s and 1930s no longer learned how to put together tops or to quilt them. She no longer stayed in her father's house waiting for "Mr. Right" to come along. Young women worked outside their parents' households, and did not have time or the interest to make bedding they could buy with the money they earned. During the worst years of the Depression in the thirties, quilts were made with colors so muted that even new quilts looked faded and patterns seemed to lack vitality. They reflected the sadly restricted lives many people lived during those years.

What little was left of the old quilting traditions was almost completely destroyed by the coming of the Second World War. Older women working as volunteers in the Red Cross made what were called "comfort quilts." The women took no more pride or satisfaction in their manufacture than in rolling bandages. They simply sewed together—by machine, if possible—pattern pieces precut through several thicknesses of fabrics selected by the Red Cross. Deviations in pattern and color were not permitted, in order to save cloth,[6] and quilting was kept to a minimum to save time and thread. These dull quilts were shipped to overseas hospitals or to people who had lost their homes when the bombs fell. In some areas throughout the country, however, church groups made colorful quilts to send overseas, sometimes using handsome quilt tops rescued from trunks and blanket boxes.

Living in their parents' homes for the duration of the war, young married women, who had never learned to quilt in the first place, were completely uninterested in making bedding for homes they might never have and husbands who might never return. Still, traditions were not completely dead. Sometime in the late 1940s, my mother-in-law, in a low tone, told me how disgraceful it was that the mother of her other daughter-in-law had let her marry without a single quilt to her name.

Tree of Paradise: quilt, pieced; cotton; red and white; Prince Edward County, Ontario, 4th quarter 19th century. W. 160 cm, L. 193 cm (63, 76 in.). The Tree of Paradise is one of the most handsome designs of the 19th century. [C.C.F.C.S.]

✿

Apple Orchard: quilt, appliquéd: cotton; sculptured quilting; designed by Ada Torrance, Orillia, Ontario, 1977. W. 231.1 cm, L. 215.9 cm (91, 85 in.). Agnes Etherington Art Centre, Queen's University. Gift of Margaret Rhodes, 1990.

✲

This was not very tactful, since I myself had only one quilt, which my elderly great-aunt had insisted on making for my wartime wedding.

After the war some church groups continued to make practical quilts to give away to those in need. I remember one such group, which insisted that the quilts must not be too pretty lest the free acquisition of desirable items encourage idleness among indigent people.

Those who enjoyed making quilts continued to do so, but it was discouraging when even members of the family didn't really want old-fashioned quilts. Most daughters and daughters-in-law preferred to buy easily washed, crinkled cotton spreads for everyday use, and shiny satin affairs for good use.

After the war, in the late forties and fifties, there seemed to be little general interest in quilt making. Old quilts lay forgotten in blanket boxes, and their owners didn't know what to do with them. During spring housecleanings, one would see them flying high on clotheslines, as sadly outdated as the old Union Jack is today. Most people hesitate to wash a fine quilt since it never looks quite the same again, but some, like the fragile Fallowfield quilt (p. 39), were washed routinely once a year, although they were never used.

The doldrums continued. In the middle fifties I went to a farm auction where a box of quilts was put up for sale. I had no intention of acquiring quilts, since I could use only expendable bedspreads now that I had young children, a dog, and a tomcat whose nighttime battles resulted in bloodstained bedcovers.

First the auctioneer pulled out a brilliant Rose of Sharon top (p. 40), unwashed and unquilted. Nobody bid. Well, I thought, it is just a top. He put it aside and held up a magnificent, unused Full Blown Tulip (p. 40), unfaded in color, finely quilted and edged. Again no one bid. There were other quilts in the box, and in disgust the auctioneer offered the whole boxful, sight unseen. Still no response. It seemed such a shame that I timidly said two dollars to start the bidding. Nobody else spoke, and I walked away with my box of quilts.

Throughout the early sixties I began to use the less important quilts as bedspreads, and to store in blanket boxes the best ones, which I still could not bring myself to use. Relatives, noticing my interest in quilts, began to give me ones they no longer used. It was somewhere in that decade that people began to talk about quilts. The Great Revival had begun. Women were making quilts again. Modern quilt makers are an enthusiastic lot. I have spoken with some who say they can barely leave their quilting long enough at noon to nab a bite of lunch in the kitchen.

Meanwhile, the few dedicated quilters who quilted quietly throughout the dark ages continued to preserve the traditions and study the rhythmic magic of design, color, and texture (p. 41). In the sixties, church groups and guilds found themselves inundated with enthusiastic women who had just discovered what the quilt makers had known all along: making quilts is fun, and the work is deeply satisfying; it fulfills the need for aesthetic expression. Old patterns were adapted by experienced quilters for use on the oversized beds that became fashionable in the latter half of the twentieth century. The circle comes around, as the very large beds that had been used in the years before 1820 gave way to smaller beds that continued to be used until 1950.

Modern quilt makers put much thought into picking fabrics to suit the pattern they have selected and working out harmonious color schemes. Usually the craftsmanship of these quilts is superb. Some young women, interested in quilt making as an artistic expression, prefer to work alone and are not reticent about showing their feelings, their hopes and disappointments, in their quilts.

Another school of quilt makers became interested in sewing quilts that are seldom used on beds but are hung on walls. These are in essence paintings in cloth, and there is nothing traditional in their startlingly beautiful designs.

Elderly quilt makers are concerned that many young women are interested only in making tops, and wonder who is going to do the quilting when the old guard is gone. Quilting is an art in itself, not simply a routine task. Only people who have been sewing by hand since childhood—and not all of them—have the dexterity to make the fine, even stitches essential in intricate quilting designs.

Quilts have become so popular that they are now being manufactured—hand-quilted—and sold in many stores. Although the patterns are colorful and more or less traditional, the quilting is not fine and the uneven stitches are sometimes crooked, perhaps to emphasize that the quilting was done by hand. What these quilts cannot give their owners is the sense of pride that is apparent in the most poorly made quilt sewn at home. The satisfaction of looking at a quilt one has made cannot be bought at a store.

Jack in the Pulpit, or Toad in the Puddle: quilt, pieced; cotton; Lennox and Addington County, Ontario, ca. 1860. W. 170 cm, L. 208 cm (67, 82 in.). A medley of red cotton prints on a buff background. [C.C.F.C.S.]

✧

Three Tulips in a Pot: quilt, appliquéd; cotton; made by Mrs. John Laurier, Gatineau Point, Quebec, 1st quarter 20th century, W. 173 cm, L. 195 cm (68, 77 in.). Very fine echo quilting and workmanship. By the 1920s floral patterns were becoming more realistic. [P.C.]

✧

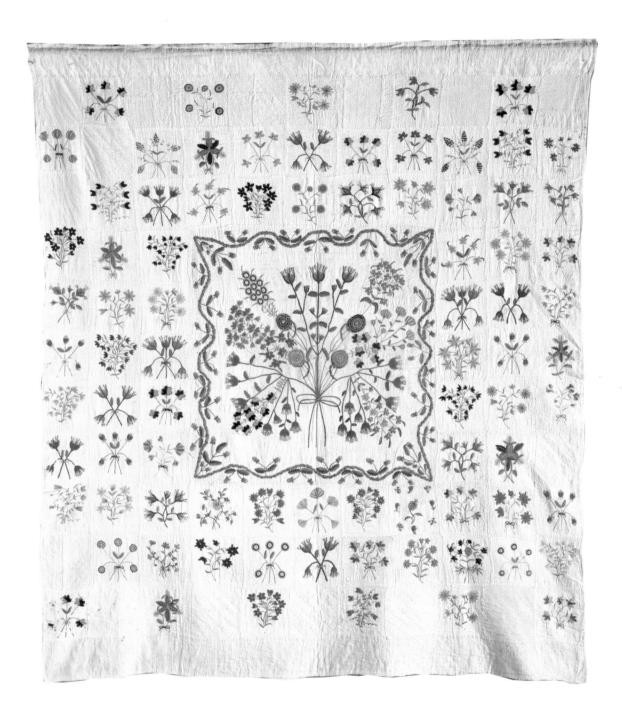

The Fallowfield Quilt: central medallion, wool embroidery on linen; Fallowfield area, Ontario, after 1820. W. 177.8 cm, L. 199.4 cm (70, 78 in.). Georgian delicacy and restraint pervade this wool, crewel-embroidered, sampler quilt. The wools are home dyed and handspun. The background material is handwoven linen. It is a summer quilt, with no filling. Agnes Etherington Art Centre, Queen's University.

✿

Rose of Sharon: quilt, appliquéd; cotton; Lanark County, Ontario, 3rd quarter 19th century. W. 155 cm, L. 217 cm (61, 85 in.). This lively version of an old favorite was quilted in 1965. [C.C.F.C.S.]

✡

Full Blown Tulip: quilt, pieced; cotton; yellow, buff (probably faded green), on white background; Lanark County, Ontario, 4th quarter 19th century. W. 152 cm, L. 190 cm (60, 75 in.). An intricate pattern because of the curved lines. [C.C.F.C.S.]

✡

Sampler Quilt: pieced; cotton and polycottons; made by the Kingston Heirloom Quilters, Kingston, Ontario, 1982. W. 248 cm, L. 214 cm (97.5, 84.5 in.). Each block of this quilt is designed and signed by its maker. Agnes Etherington Art Centre, Queen's University.

✪

CHAPTER 2

The Quilting Bee and the Marriage Bed

If several young gentlemen receive an invitation to a tea, they may be assured that their services are required at a quilting-bee, which often is followed by courtship and matrimony. Indeed it is one of the methods taken by the Canadian cupid to ensnare hearts and provide work for Hymen.

—Samuel Strickland, *Twenty-Seven Years in Canada West*

ALTHOUGH A GREAT DEAL OF WORK WAS accomplished in one day at a quilting bee, it was above all great fun. Often it was the only occasion a woman had much chance to talk and laugh with friends. Hopeful young women who, since their childhoods, had been making quilt tops for their eventual marriages were eager to meet young men. A bee was a rare opportunity for young people to strike up friendships that frequently led to romances.

In rural areas, where most people lived in the early years of settlement, the women of a family pieced together several tops during the fall and winter, and in the late winter or early spring, before the plowing and seeding season began, a quilting party or bee would be held to quilt the lot. This was important when a young woman was planning marriage and needed the quilts for her new household.

At a well-organized quilting bee the workers, often accompanied by children, came early in the afternoon, and in the late afternoons after the chores were done, husbands and young men arrived in time for supper, followed by a party, probably with fiddle music and dancing. Mothers encouraged daughters to become good quilters so that they would be

OPPOSITE PAGE:
Birds in Flight Quilt: embroidered, central medallion surrounded by wide borders of red flying birds represented by triangles; red cotton on white; linen back; made by Jega Matilda Garland, Glenburnie, Ontario, 18?0 (the third numeral is unclear). W. 202 cm, L. 198 cm, (80, 78 in.). A beautiful, happy quilt, preserved by her relatives. [P.C.] (See detail p. 65)

asked to all the bees, where they would meet young men. As it turned out, however, the good quilters were expected to remain in the parlor quilting, while those who did not sew so fine a seam were sent to the kitchen to help with the refreshments. Although mothers might consider this a disgrace, the situation had its advantages, since the eligible young men gathered in the kitchen to await supper and the party. This gave the rejected seamstresses first chance at prospective suitors. Alas, it was not the number of stitches a girl made to the inch that interested the young men!

Most accounts of early quilting bees stress this social aspect. A "Canuck" in *Pen Pictures of Early Pioneer Life in Upper Canada* describes an early quilting bee, which, like most bees of the period, seems to be rather boisterous:

> A number of the ladies, both married and single would gather at a friend's house where the bee was to be held, mostly early in the afternoon to do the quilting. The husbands and young men were invited to tea, after which the time was spent in social conversation and popular diversions, the young folk engaging in the various games and amusements which were then the fashion at the time. Cupid was then just as busy and active with his bow and quiver as he is now and has ever and always been, and the young men were not one whit behind the young men of today in paying their devoirs to the pretty girls in the company. The so-called kissing games were quite popular as might be expected. It was the custom at these bees for the girls to throw a quilt when finished over one of the young men and laugh to see him extricate himself. Sometimes too they would succeed in getting one of the party enveloped in the quilt, when with a strong hand at each corner, they would toss them high in the air. This added greatly to the mirth and jollification of the occasion.[7]

Whether on a back-country farm or in the more elegant drawing room of the Stricklands, the message was the same. Young women making quilts were looking for young men with whom they might share their bedcovers—within, of course, the bonds of Holy Matrimony.

Although making the tops over a long period did not call for much of a cash outlay, a considerable amount of money was needed when it was time to purchase the materials necessary to complete the entire twelve quilts required for a marriage. As a result, the finishing of the quilts was usually left until a marriage was imminent. Money was the scarcest commodity of all, and needles, thread, fabric for backing the quilts, and cotton bats for fillings had to be bought at the store. If the family had sheep, the women carded wool into bats to save on expense. Some quilts were stuffed with loose wool and tied.

Although unbleached cotton was sometimes purchased to use on the backs, most quilts were backed with the cotton bags in which flour and sugar were bought by the hundredweight. These bags were of good-quality cotton that improved with each washing and lasted longer than most store-bought fabrics. Although new cloth was sometimes purchased for the marriage or good quilt, everyday quilts were made from scraps of cloth left over from the cutting of clothing. Because clothing for the customarily large families was made at home, the rag bags of such families were generous ones, providing a quilt maker with a riotous wealth of textures, printed designs, and a great diversity of colors. Remnants were frequently traded among the families in a neighborhood, giving the quilt maker an even more varied palette.

So much work went into the making of quilts that a woman did not like to employ used materials unless she had no choice. A woman in Durham County, Ontario, composed an entire Star of Bethlehem quilt, containing twelve lively stars, from discarded coats and other heavy woolen materials (p. 46). The result is so vivacious that one wonders if, as she made the quilt, she was thinking of "when the morning stars sang together, and the sons of man shouted for joy."[8]

After her marriage, the special quilt made by a young woman for use on her marriage bed would become her good quilt, reserved for special occasions. If possible, the cloth used in this quilt was bought at the store rather than recycled from the rag bag. Although a young woman's everyday quilt tops were usually quilted at a bee, the wedding quilt was quilted by the prospective bride, her mother, and perhaps a few relatives or friends.

Because this quilt required an outlay of cash, young women sometimes went to the city to work as domestic servants for a time in order to accumulate money to buy fabrics to make the wedding quilt and clothing. Other young women worked overtime at home, churning butter to barter for cloth at the local store. Fathers were heard to comment that the cows were relieved when the wedding was over.

Star of Bethlehem: quilt, 12 pieced stars; assorted woolens; Durham County, Ontario, 4th quarter 19th century. W. 157 cm, L. 212 cm (62, 83 in.). In spite of the fact that this quilt is composed of discarded coats and other heavy materials, a lively and vivacious result was achieved. [C.C.F.C.S]

Older women sometimes made a second good quilt—or even more if they could afford to buy the cloth—after their children were grown and they had less work to do. The granddaughter of Betsey Dodge, of Grenville County, Ontario, remembers her family telling how Grandma and the hired girl sat down on winter afternoons "when the snow was blowing" to quilt because they enjoyed it so much. Together they made several beautiful quilts, each one decorated with vines, flowers, birds, and a weeping willow in fine, freehand quilting.

Traditional bees became scarcer toward the end of the nineteenth

century. Church groups began to take over the role played by neighborhood gatherings, but women still met in little groups to quilt when
bedding was needed in a hurry. A woman in Frontenac County,
Ontario, told me of moving as a bride into the family homestead of
her young husband. The mother of the family had died several years
earlier, and there were not enough bedcovers left to keep the family
members warm:

> "Of course I had my own," she said, "but they were not nearly enough
> to go around. Almost the first thing I did was to get the men to take me
> to the store to buy print and some unbleached cotton and some bats,
> and I worked every moment I could spare making up quilt tops. After
> they were ready, my sister, and my sister-in-law and I sat down and quilt-
> ed day after day. I made simple patterns and used my sewing machine all
> I could to speed things up. It made me so happy to see nice, warm quilts
> on all those beds."

I remember being present at a twentieth-century quilting bee. It was
one in which I played an inglorious role. My mother had decided to
make her children a red-and-white circus quilt, for which she had bought
a pattern. During the summer she sat on the veranda or in her chair by
the south window, embroidering and appliquéing for some weeks, and
when the blocks were finished and sewn together, she asked a few
women to the house to help with the quilting. Great-Aunt Maggie was
invited to come in from the farm for a few days' visit and Mother, with
her usual diplomacy, asked Auntie to oversee the work. This presented
no difficulties because Auntie, supremely confident in her role as expert
quilt maker, would probably have done so anyway. She helped Mother
set up the quilting frame in the parlor, where it almost filled the small
room, and the two women "put in," or attached, the three layers of the
quilt to the quilting frame to hold them taut while they were stitching.
The quilting designs were now ready to be marked with pale-blue chalk
to guide the quilters. Mother's long-time friend Nell Barry, a traveling
dressmaker whom we children dearly loved, came to stay, as well. In
addition, Mrs. Walsh and Mrs. McMillan, who lived in the village,
stopped by in the afternoons. It was a small group, but all the room
would hold.

That first evening, when it was too dim to sew, my brother and I, both too young to go to school, played bear in the dark cave beneath the stretched quilt until we became wildly excited. The next morning, I helped carry a good many items from the kitchen into the parlor to use in the marking: water glasses, handleless teacups, saucers, wooden potato pounders, heart-shaped and leaf-shaped cookie cutters, and the dinner plates used to mark what is sometimes called the fan pattern. While the women were preparing to begin the marking, I crawled under the quilt. Feeling recklessly safe in my lair, I began to tip glasses and cups and move the carefully arranged dinner plates. This brought a speedy end to my first quilting bee.

After a few days the quilt was finished. The women took it out from the frame, and Auntie shook it vigorously a few times.

"First we bounce the cat on it for luck," Miss Barry announced firmly. "Whoever he runs to will be the first one married."

There were four spinsters and one widow in the quilting party, counting me and the hired girl who was viewing the finished quilt with me. Mother picked up our good-natured White Puss, placed her carefully on the new quilt, and then the four women pulled it taut to bounce her. When Puss jumped, they all said she ran to me, but I knew they just said that to make me feel good after my disgrace, because Puss dashed straight to old Granny McMillan.

At early quilting bees, spirits ran high, especially when the quilts were being finished for a wedding. No one was allowed to forget that the quilts were intended for use on the bed of a newly married young couple, and that thought led to mirthful remarks, among the women especially in the afternoon session when no men were present. The prospect of a marriage meant that the community was growing. Men and women looked forward to an increase in the population when those quilts were in use on the bed. As the afternoon drew to a close, the men in the kitchen kept slipping out to the barn at intervals to refresh themselves with a wee drop of the whiskey that was being kept out of sight until after supper. By the time the fiddlers tuned up, the whiskey jug had made its appearance on the kitchen table. Jokes about the intended use of the quilts became more ribald as the evening progressed. Even strait-laced matrons smirked behind hands held over their mouths and modest maidens blushed and giggled.

In early years the bed was often the most important and expensive piece of furniture in the house. In the village I came from, it was said that the only possessions a young couple really needed to begin married life were a bed and a stove. During the Depression, in the thirties, the priest would buy the bedstead if it was necessary to expedite a marriage.

Beds are still important in our lives, but in early years, before people moved around so much, the bed a young woman was making quilts for was the place where her marriage would be consummated, where her babies would be born, and where she would die when her time came. A woman making bedcovers for her future life was preparing for a career, one that would keep her occupied for the next fifty years and, if she was successful, would ensure her happiness and contentment for life.

As a result, the making of a bride's quilt was serious business. Into her bridal quilt a young woman sewed her dreams of romance, of long life, of immortality, and, though rarely mentioned, her hopes for a passionate bedfellow. Young women of the previous century may not have known all the details, but most of them had the general picture. They had read the Song of Solomon, talked to friends, and had a good idea what went on beneath those red roses on the coverlet, and they were prepared to enjoy it.

Quilts reflected the various crises in a woman's life. Sometimes a woman set up a frame and quilted alone in her spare time. Sitting by herself after the children were in bed, she was bound to think about a husband who was not home that night, although he should have been, and her worries showed in her quilt. Sometimes a woman looking at a completed quilt could see a section where her stitches were uneven and crooked. Someone else might not even notice, but she would recall how her eyes had kept filling with tears that evening so that she could barely see where the needle was. That was all water under the bridge now, but both she and the quilt remembered.

When the colors in a quilt are soft grays and silvers and muted blues, it was probably made by a worried woman in a season of discontent. On the other hand, when brilliant red birds, represented by triangles, fly off wildly in all directions, it is safe to speculate that the quilt maker was probably a happy young woman being courted that season by an ardent beau.

CHAPTER 3

The Quilt Makers

*It is a token of healthy and gentle characteristics, when
women of high thoughts and accomplishments live to sew;
especially as they are never more at home with their own
hearts than while so occupied.*

—Nathaniel Hawthorne, *The Marble Faun*

MANY OF THE WOMEN I TALKED TO ABOUT
making quilts were quilting in the days when making warm
bedcovers was an essential daily chore, as routine as baking
bread and sweeping the floor. In the stove-heated, uninsulated houses in
which they lived, warm quilts were always needed. Very little heat
reached the upper story at any time, and during the night stoves burned
very slowly, often going out altogether. When one first climbed into bed,
bedclothes were like sheets of ice, and during a cold spell two wool blankets topped with two or three quilts were not too many. No one complained of the weight of quilts on nights when the water in the pitcher on
the washstand froze before morning. Women knew their quilts were
appreciated, and they lived in an era when most women took pride and
some took pleasure in their chosen role as housewife.

Almost invariably, these women distinguished between "real" quilt
makers and those who just made quilts. They would proudly give me
the names of the "real" quilt makers in the community and suggest I
would enjoy a talk with them. The quilt makers they referred to made
quilts because they liked doing so, whether or not bedding was needed.
My informants would tell me, "It was, you might say, their hobby, and
they always made better quilts than the rest of us."

When I met these quilt makers, I found that such a weak word as
hobby was scarcely adequate to describe an activity that was a consuming

OPPOSITE PAGE:
*Velvet Sampler;
quilt, pieced with
embroidered outlines;
velvet; made by Amelia
Crozier, Switzerville
Road, Ontario, 1939.
This charming and
unique quilt sparkles
with life and color,
although the designs
are naively drawn.*
[P.C.]

✡

passion with them. Most women of their generation felt guilty if they were enjoying themselves, but quilting was an acceptable pleasure because it was utilitarian. Several of these quilt makers were old and frail, and some were bedridden. They no longer made quilts, but their enthusiasm in talking about them had not dimmed. Although in many cases their eyesight was almost gone, it was obvious these elderly women could see, in their minds' eyes, glorious, glowing images of their past creations. Sometimes the thin, knotted fingers would move a little, as if they were again feeling the fine rows of stitching in the cloth. A few, more fortunate, women were still making quilts. One woman well into her nineties showed me an intricate Eastern Star she had just sewn. When an elderly woman is asked to date her quilts, she proudly inscribes her age rather than the year the quilt was made.

By the second quarter of the twentieth century, inexpensive factory-produced blankets good enough for every day were available in stores or could be ordered easily by country people from mail-order catalogs. By that time making quilts was no longer an economic necessity in most households, but many women, especially those in rural areas, kept up this work for several years. At leisurely meetings of church or community groups, often held in the comfortable houses of the members, hard-working women, always conscious of the endless tasks awaiting them on their return home, felt less idle if they worked with their hands while they sat talking. "It gives me something to do," a woman would say in an era, fast disappearing, when "the devil found work for idle hands to do."

Some of these "real" quilt makers were artists who took as much pride and joy in their cloth creations as do artists who paint on canvas with oils. Except for some early quilts sewn by our pioneer women, which I will be discussing in chapter 5, most quilts are made from standard patterns taken from pattern books. But individual women interpret the same patterns differently. Dull quilts are made by unimaginative women, while those gifted with an uncanny ability to manipulate color and design use patterns only to serve their convenience (p. 54).

Frequently, nineteenth-century women who never married were excellent quilt makers. Not all of them had that inborn sense of color and design essential in a "real" quilt maker, but they did have almost unlimited time and undivided interest, and above all the endless patience needed to attend to the tedious details of the quilt's construction. In the nineteenth century, these were luxuries that the average married woman, who usually became pregnant every second year of her reproductive life, did not have. Spinsters, even those who worked like unpaid servants in the busy households of their relatives, had more time to work on quilts than did their married sisters.

During her girlhood, a woman made the customary twelve quilts to have ready when she moved into her own home. If that day did not arrive, she generally kept those quilts unused in her blanket box, although she continued to make quilts, both for use in the household in which she lived and to give to countless relatives. As a result, some of those unused quilts are among the few pieced quilts made for everyday use that have survived in good condition.

By the second half of the nineteenth century, enthusiastic quilt makers began to enter their best quilts in the annual county fairs. For several nights before each fair, the glittering prospect of the coveted first prize haunted the dreams of ambitious quilt makers. Often the awarding of prizes by the judges engendered an intense rivalry among quilt makers. In a small community a surprising number of judges were related to, or were old friends of, the parents of the winners, and criticism could be stinging. Telephone conversations on rural party lines criticizing the utter selfishness of a winner who continued year after year to show the same prize-winning quilt would become so heated that the wires almost melted. People used to say that the swallows left early each year because their feet were burning by fair time.

The bitterness was confined to a relatively small group of select quilt makers who were not overburdened with modesty. Strangely enough, women "who just made quilts" seemed to be without envy and admired with unstinting generosity the abilities of "real" quilt makers in selecting subtle colors and harmonizing textures in cloth.

After 1930 or so, a quilt was made primarily to fulfill an ornamental role, and it was often used as a bedspread, under which no one was allowed to sleep; or was kept folded in a blanket box, to be brought out only for show. The day of the unmarried woman who devoted much of her time to making quilts was over, as well. If young women decided to remain single, they left their parents' homes and found employment elsewhere.

Outstanding quilts were and are the outcome of hours of careful planning. My great-aunt Maggie was both a spinster and a quilt maker

*Little Houses: quilt,
pieced; printed
cottons; Picton,
Ontario, ca. 1890.
W. 168 cm, L. 210 cm
(66, 83 in.). Forty-two
little houses, and no
two made with
identical fabrics. [P.C.]*
☼

of the first water. When I was a child, I watched her select scraps of fabrics from the rag bag and arrange them on the roomy apron covering her generous knees. She would sort and rearrange the tiny pieces of cloth, changing their proximity over and over.

"It isn't only what each color is," she would tell me. "It's what this color looks like beside that color. You have to use your mind's eye to see the whole thing finished."

During the next stage, she would place several unseamed blocks of the prospective quilt on the kitchen table and keep varying the colors and textures again and again until the entire quilt was displayed to her satisfaction, before she sewed a single seam. Auntie, the only woman in her household, augmented the contents of her rather meager rag bag from time to time by buying cotton prints from the Montreal pedlar who came regularly to her door, tempting her with fabrics she was unable to resist.

Most women enjoyed making quilts whether they were "real" quilt makers or not. They took pride and satisfaction in their achievement when the finished product, now an entity rather than a conglomeration of parts, was taken out of the quilting frame and held up for all to see. Off the frame, it could be admired for the first time without the distraction of needles and threads and open seams, and one could see and feel the exciting raised textures created on the surface by the various quilting designs. At that moment, even the most modest and unassuming woman knew she was an artist, and that she was looking at a masterpiece. Even a simple everyday pattern can undergo a magic transformation by a clever choice of color, while a slight shift in design can convert a utilitarian bedcover into an enchanted creation.

My mother made very few quilts in her lifetime and could not truly be described as a "real" quilt maker or even someone who just made quilts, but I can still see the glory on her face when her circus quilt, the one finished at her only quilting bee, was spread on a bed for the first time. A large elephant standing in front of an embroidered tent was appliquéd on the generous central block. The other blocks, each containing an embroidered circus animal, formed a wide border up the sides and across the ends. Wide strips of red cotton made up the set that separated and framed the blocks. We laughed when White Puss jumped up to investigate the unfamiliar animals and sniff the stalwart red elephant in the center. It was such a chunky, solid, endearing elephant, weighing down the quilt so that there was no danger, even on the coldest night, of the bedcovers slipping to the floor.

In later years, Mother made another circus quilt for a grandson, using the same pattern but elongating the design so that the side blocks appeared at the ends, adding to the length. The seal with a ball on its nose and the running zebra now lay across the pillows. At the time the original quilt was made, pillows were placed on top of the quilt, but when the second quilt was made, it was stylish to conceal the pillows. Unfortunately, this change of shape meant that the elephant no longer stood in the exact center of the quilt. This shift in the balance of the design, combined with the insipid blue and yellow colors, now more fashionable than the startling red and white of the original, resulted in a disappointing bedcover.

Ideally, a "real" quilt maker should create a quilt of outstanding design every time, accentuated with an array of glowing, harmonizing colors; it should be made in materials whose textures augment the originality of the pattern's interpretation. Above all—or at least as important, in many eyes—is the workmanship: the care taken with the details; the skillfully executed, unpuckered corners and well-planned borders. And then there is the pinnacle of achievement, the quilting, the ultimate in excellence and perfection. Stitches must all be the same size and tension. The quilting designs must emphasize the pattern as well as create beautiful pictures on their own. The surface of a good quilt ripples like sea-washed sand.

There are, and always have been, quilt makers who are so interested in the visual impact of a quilt that they lack patience or simply don't care about tedious details such as mitered corners and perfectly piped bindings. Some quilt in a hurry, so eager to get the quilt done that they overlook slight imperfections. Yet often the magic is still present. The velvet quilt (p. 50) sparkles with life and color, although the motifs that the quilt maker

Old Fashioned Basket: quilt, appliquéd (flowers) and pieced (baskets); quilting: various cottons and polycottons; made by Quilters of Princess Street United Church, Kingston, Ontario, 1985. W. 210 cm, L. 178 cm (83, 70 in.). Agnes Etherington Art Centre, Queen's University. Gift of the Quilters of Princess Street United Church.

✿

has pieced and embroidered on each block are crudely executed. The quilt gives the impression that the maker, who was an artist in fabrics, cared little for painstaking details as long as the work resulted in the picture she carried in her mind. It is equally true that a number of quilts that are perfect in every detail lack the spark of creative originality. Old Fashioned Basket (p. 55) is a good example of a perfect quilt.

A quilt maker in Frontenac County, Ontario, who came from a long line of expert quilt makers, insisted that "the old people" always said a really good quilt must be the work of only one pair of hands—possibly two—so that there would not be different styles of quilting. With a shrug she added, "With all them women working and talking like crazy at the same time, you can imagine what kind of a quilt you get."

While there are important exceptions, it is generally thought that only practical everyday bedcovers can be quilted by several people working together on the same quilt. The exceptions include certain church groups or guilds whose members work together week in, week out, and seem to accommodate one another's styles, or else they are all such skilled quilters that there are no noticeable differences in their work. The Kingston Heirloom Quilters, Kingston, Ontario, are a group who work together so well that they work almost as one woman.

A few women cared little or nothing about the aesthetic appearance of their bedcovers. I have been to country auctions where tables and sofas were piled high with quilts, and although the quilts were soundly made and well cared for, not one of them was worth looking at twice. Certainly no one would take that type of quilt home to photograph and cherish. Those quilts were bought by fortunate old bachelors who probably never wore them out with washing but slept snug and warm beneath them the rest of their days. Quilts like those fulfill the purpose for which they were made. They are never seen again, and we forget that all quilts of the nineteenth and early twentieth centuries were not works of art or even pleasing to the eye.

Quilts were meant to be used, and those faded and worn a bit are still appealing to the eye. The colors of the little pieces of prints run into one another, achieving a new harmony. New quilts can never quite emulate the subtlety of hue that is acquired through age and use with the slight yellowing of the whites and the faint softening of the colors. Unfortunately, the arrival of the washing machine in most households made cleaning quilts too easy, and the result was the speedy deterioration and eventual discarding of many good quilts. No quilt can tolerate constant washing. In the early days, because of the difficulty of handling so much wet, bulky cloth, care was taken to postpone the day when washing was unavoidable. Such heavy items were likely allowed to become somewhat more soiled at a time when the subdued light cast by candles and coal-oil lamps covered a multitude of sins. The arrival of electric lights in the twentieth century changed the housekeeping practices in many households. I have heard aging relatives bewail the necessity of sweeping the kitchen floor after supper now that they had "the lights."

It is probably safe to say that most quilts we see hanging in museums and illustrated in books today were made by "real" quilt makers, and most of them are "good" appliquéd quilts. Appliquéd quilts, never common, were always valued more, and mothers passed them down to daughters, with dire warnings about their care. Because their superior monetary worth has always been recognized, both by their makers and subsequent owners, they were washed less often and treated with great respect. As a result, their survival rate is higher than that of pieced everyday quilts, no matter how attractive they were. Artistic quilt makers made everyday quilts, too, and some of those were masterpieces.

When making an appliquéd quilt, it was traditional to choose a fashionable pattern and buy new cloth for the purpose. This limited the choice of colors, because additional hues increased the cost. Also, when making a good quilt a quilt maker was restricted in her artistic expression by the possible disapproval of her peers. She dared not stray too far from the conventional when making a bedcover that would be on display for the rest of her life and probably survive her. But when she was making an everyday quilt, the venturous quilt maker could choose from the large selection of colors and fabrics in the rag bag. And because the quilt would be seen only by the family, she was freer to express her artistic talents. If the quilt was not a success, it would eventually wear out and be discarded anyway. Nor was there any chance that an unconventional quilt would appear on the guest bed for the members of the Ladies Aid Society to see when taking off their coats. If it did, the nonconforming quilt maker could be certain that the wildly innovative color scheme and odd design of her new quilt would be the subject of uncharitable discussion and mirth up and down the concession road at supper tables that night.

CHAPTER 4

Quilt Patterns, Their Meanings and Origins

O swallow, sister, O changing swallow…
Sing, while the hours and the wild birds follow,
Take flight and follow and find the sun.

—Swinburne, *Itylus*

IN GENERAL, THE SUBJECTS OF NINETEENTH-century quilts reflect the daily experiences of the women who made them. Women often found their inspiration in the natural world around them—the birds, the trees, the flowers, even the fields and fences. This was especially true in everyday quilts, where the thrifty quilt maker followed pieced patterns in order to make use of scraps of assorted materials. On the other hand, in the making of appliquéd quilts, which were the usual choice for marriage and other good quilts, fashionable patterns were preferred.

It is probable that most patterns had their origins in times when signs or tokens placed on everyday objects had symbolic meanings. It is, therefore, impossible to discuss patterns of quilts without becoming involved in symbolism, although the original meanings of the symbolic designs were almost forgotten in the nineteenth century and ignored in the twentieth.

According to the beliefs of the old earth-based religions, such as Druidism, every object in nature—birds, trees, bushes, flowers, rocks, lakes, mountains—had spirits living within them, some good, some evil. People who had little control of their own destinies believed implicitly in the constant presence of those spirits. Spirits were continually battling to control the souls of those living in the household. They hovered around

OPPOSITE PAGE:
Log Cabin, Straight Furrow: quilt, pieced; plain, earth-colored woolens; conspicuous red hearths; Renfrew County, Ontario, 4th quarter 19th century. W. 163 cm, L. 191 cm (64, 75 in.). Simple, naive interpretation of a pattern. [C.C.F.C.S.]

✿

the bedstead, since the soul was especially vulnerable when it wandered during sleep, or was in a state of transition during the hours of birth and death. In the marriage bed, spirits influenced the chances of conception, which was of prime importance in those days when old people relied on younger members of the family for support and physical safety. For these reasons, the bedcover was a natural repository for symbols of procreation and birth.

These beliefs were not altogether abandoned by all people when Christianity was introduced. Primitive people who worshipped rocks and trees simply incorporated their old beliefs in the new religion. Beliefs as strong as these were not easily forgotten or abandoned, and cautious people continued to maintain a foothold in both religions.

Very early quilted counterpanes, made and used in the British Isles, France, Germany, and several other countries were sewn of one length of cloth and relied on elaborate quilting designs for decorative effect. These designs reveal a wealth of symbolism: suns, stars, swirling rosettes, intricate lovers' knots, diamond shapes, unbroken flowering vines, twisted ropes—all had important symbolic meanings. It is likely that in less prosperous households where cloth was scarce, the same designs were made by cutting scraps of leftover cloth into shapes that made coverlet tops when sewn together, like the pieced quilts we see today. The oak leaf, for example, signified long life since the oak tree is tough and enduring. The diamond shape, with its female imagery, stands for procreation and therefore fertility. The swirling rosette, a commonly used quilting design in early coverlets, is a turning circle representing life without end. Windmill blades, which appear in a large variety of pieced patterns of various names, repeat the same message of never-ending life.

From early times the swallow was considered a symbol of new life. In Christianity it is also a symbol of the coming of the Holy Ghost, the return of life in springtime, as well as the Resurrection. During the Middle Ages it was believed that swallows buried themselves in the mud in wintertime and were resurrected in the spring. A renewal of faith was felt when they reappeared.

In the nineteenth century, although the ancient traditional patterns were still being used, occasionally with symbolic significance, women were beginning to forget the original meanings, and the same subjects merely expressed images encountered in their daily lives.

Birds in Flight: quilt, pieced; cotton; Portsmouth Village, Ontario, 4th quarter 19th century. W. 155 cm, L. 184 cm (61, 72 in.). The stylized birds are placed in diagonal rows across the quilt, larger and spaced more widely in the center as the birds approach, and smaller and closer together in the far corners as they fade away. [C.C.F.C.S.]

In early quilt patterns, a flying bird is represented by a triangle. Several flying bird patterns were commonly used: Birds in Flight, Birds in the Air, Birds in Paradise, Birds in a Tree, as well as many swallow patterns: Swallow in the Path, Swallows in the Window, Chimney Swallows, Swallow's Flight, Swallow's Nest, among others. Perhaps hard-working housewives of the nineteenth century envied the birds their freedom. Birds could go where they wished effortlessly, were without encumbrances, were filled with joy and without feelings of guilt. Rural people are still fascinated with the exultant flight of the swallow and feel an affection for this particular bird because it nests so close to people. Only people living in cold, lonely farmhouses can truly experience the surge of joy that arises in the heart when the swallows return in the spring.

Mary Ellen Wood who lived on the shores of Lake Ontario made a remarkable Birds in Flight quilt (p. 61). She probably watched the arrivals and departures of the great flocks of birds as they flew across the lake, small in the distance as they approached, larger overhead, then smaller and smaller again as they disappeared once more in the distance.

The goose was another popular quilt motif (p. 64). During the Renaissance the domestic goose was considered the symbol of providence and vigilance, and people have continued to look on this bird with affection. Quilts with goose patterns probably give people a feeling of comfort and safety. The feathers of the gray goose provided people with comfortable mattresses and pillows. Several generations of children were lulled to sleep with the singing of "The Old Gray Goose." Among the patterns are the Old Brown Goose, Goose in the Pond, Goose Foot in the Mud, Goose in the Window. Wild Goose Chase and Wild Geese Flying reflect the exhilaration we feel when the wild geese fly overhead in spring and fall, since they represent freedom and the call of the wilderness.

Flower patterns are usually found on good quilts, and these are sometimes appliquéd, sometimes pieced, or sometimes combine both techniques. In nineteenth-century quilts the lily, under several names— North Carolina Lily, Canada Lily, Noon Day Lily—was a favorite, possibly because of the biblical assertion that it toils not, neither does it spin, a fascinating prospect for hard-working women. Early floral patterns like Jack in the Pulpit (p. 37), and Full Blown Tulip (p. 40) are complex and stylized.

Most beloved are the Rose patterns, many of which originate from the Tudor Rose quilting pattern used for generations in the old countries. It was always a favorite marriage quilt, since the red rose was a symbol of passionate love, often referred to in verse. This pattern continued to be in use so long that the design changed and evolved several times over the years. In the last half of the nineteenth century, the rose pattern, now called the Rose of Sharon, endured as the choice for bridal quilts. Prim young women in the Victorian era were too inhibited to speak of the red rose as a symbol of passion, but they were able to accept the pattern when it was called the Rose of Sharon, which derived its name from the Song of Solomon[9] in the Bible. The obvious sexual symbols in the Song of Solomon can be interpreted as representative of Christ's love for the Church.

The flowering bush or tree, symbolic of the Tree of Life, is commonly found on marriage quilts, and there are many related tree patterns: Pine Tree, Cherry Tree and Birds, Little Beech Tree, Tree of Life, Tree Everlasting, Tree of Paradise, and the Tree of Temptation. Many of these names have biblical significance,[10] but the tree, especially in the Hebrides, continued to be worshipped in out-of-the-way places long after Christianity appeared. Trees were thought to house powerful spirits one did not care to offend. That this pagan belief is not entirely forgotten is sometimes revealed in quilts where the phallic symbol of the pine tree is accentuated by oversized quilted designs of twisted rope thought to represent the entwining of two lives. The repeat of this pattern is a small oval within a larger one. Used in this way, it is a unmistakable fertility symbol, which, as I mentioned before, my great-aunt always placed on marriage quilts. Less romantic souls in the early twentieth century sometimes called this pattern Pumpkin Seed, and it is possible Auntie, in all innocence, thought of it as simply pumpkin seed, instead of an overt sexual symbol. Knowing Auntie, I expect the latter meaning is precisely what she intended and would have considered entirely natural under the circumstances.

Many quilts employ a running vine around the borders as a symbol of a long and fruitful life. This symbol, too, has overtly Christian overtones, for in Christian mythology the flowering vine is a vivid metaphor for God and his people: "I am the vine, ye are the branches… He that abideth in me and I in him, the same shall bring forth much fruit…"[11] Unfortunately, in making such borders, it is difficult to round the corners

Canada Goose, Waterlilies, and Cattails: quilt, appliquéd; cotton; black and white goose, waterlilies, and cattails on green background; made by the Thousand Island Branch of the Rebecca Lodge, ca. 1930, for a raffle, Lansdowne, Ontario. W. 163 cm, L. 239 cm (64, 94 in.). This is an interesting design for a quilt of this period.
[P.C.]
✷

neatly, which sometimes breaks the continuity of the vine. Some quilt makers bypass this problem by inserting small free-standing designs in the corners. Superstitious people thought a break in the border vine signified an untimely loss of love or life.

In the first half of the nineteenth century, marriage quilts with embroidered central medallions displayed several symbols—among them flowering bushes, butterflies, and birds. Embroidery designs such as these were taught in schools for young ladies, but the designs were probably traditional ones since few Canadian girls were able to attend school at that time. The symbols are discreet and stress the religious aspects of life. Hearts quilted or embroidered in the center of a quilt indicate a marriage quilt.

A handsome woolen quilt (p. 30) was made in 1856 by Frances Mulligan, a young woman of Irish descent, who lived in a log farmhouse in the Hazeldean area of Carleton County. In the center of the quilt is an embroidered medallion surrounded by four pieced frames or borders. The outer border is composed of Nine Patch blocks—considered mystical, since in Christian mythology the number three and its multiples have to do with the Holy Trinity. The four block corners in the frames represent the world: north, south, east, and west. The central medallion contains a flowering branch growing out of an urn, an ancient symbol of the renewal

Birds in Flight Quilt detail, showing scalloped circular medallion embroidered with flowering branch in urn, butterflies, and flowers. See p.42 for entire quilt.

✡

of life. The flowers connote fruitfulness and the annual resurgence of growth. The peacocks and butterflies on the branches are symbolic, respectively, of immortality, since it was the belief that the flesh of the peacock does not decay, and of the Resurrection of Christ and, by extension, of all men. The latter meaning comes from the emergence of the butterfly from its chrysalis, its apparent tomb. The scalloped circle enclosing the central flowering branch, with its peacocks and butterflies, represents the moon, a common symbol for the female, while the running vine surrounding the circle stands for longevity. The hearts that are quilted throughout the central area show that the quilt was meant for a marriage. The quilt was made when Frances was sixteen, but she apparently died before her marriage, for the quilt was found folded in a blanket box in her father's house.

A lovely embroidered, appliquéd, and pieced quilt (pp. 26–27) was made by Mary Morris in Leeds County, Ontario, in 1826. Like Frances Mulligan, her family came from Ireland. The quilt may have a traditional design, since Mary's sister Elizabeth had an identical one, dated a year later. It is possible that Mary made Elizabeth's quilt as well as her own, since Mary, who was born with a physical handicap that prevented her

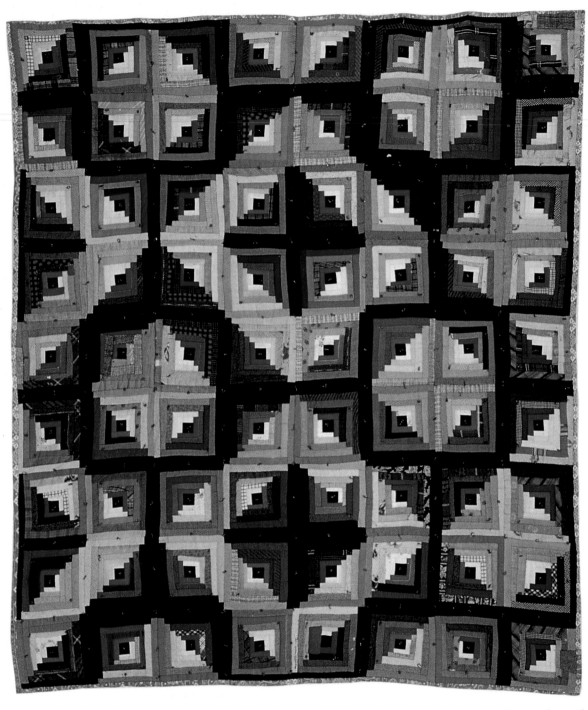

Log Cabin, Barn Raising variant: quilt, pieced; assorted silks and wools in shades of red, purple, and blue; Leeds County, Ontario, ca. 1890. W. 175 cm, L. 198 cm (69, 78 in.). This quilt maker has successfully organized a beautiful selection of harmonious colors. The handsome red calico back is typical of such quilts. [C.C.F.C.S.]

✿

from walking, was able to devote much of her time to embroidery. Elizabeth married, and her quilt shows more wear than Mary's, who did not marry. The central medallion contains the usual flowering branch, butterflies, peacocks, flowers, and a hex sign to ward off evil, but Mary has included red-coated hunters chasing deer—a scene from the old country, which Mary, who was born in Canada, could not have seen.

Another effective early quilt (pp. 42, 65) looks to have been made by a happy young woman. An embroidered medallion, which is a circle with scallops containing butterflies, roses, and a flowering bush in an urn, is surrounded by great wings of bright-red triangles, or flying birds. The name Jega Matilda Garland is embroidered in the center, along with the date February 3, 18?0. The third numeral of the year is unclear; possibly the year is 1820 or even 1840. The charming design appears to have been drawn from memory rather than copied from a pattern. This lovely quilt was acquired in Glenburnie, Ontario, from descendants of the maker.

The colorful panoramas of nature were not lost on nineteenth-century quilt makers. Log Cabin patterns were successful, nonrepresentational expressions of these difficult subjects, all rural in nature. The designs were widely employed in the late nineteenth century because they made use of the smallest scraps of fabric so that nothing was wasted.

These strong, lusty quilts are nearly always backed with colorful, handsome calicos. There is no need for stuffing, since the folded fabric provides sufficient bulk. Quilting is done sparsely around the individual squares. Log Cabin quilts are made by attaching strips of folded cloth to background squares. Certain squares are made using dark cloth, others using light, and then four squares are sewn together to make blocks in various combinations of light and dark required for the different patterns. The name Log Cabin derives from the fact that each folded strip of cloth represents a log, and each block, consisting of four squares, is a cabin. The side of the block with light colors represents the sunny wall of the cabin, and the dark side is the shaded north wall. The little red square in the center of the block is the hearth, in which the light must never go out. A few women made their quilts with darkened hearths, although it is difficult to say whether this was done deliberately.

Log Cabin quilts are rife with sexual symbols. Some are overtly sexual, such as in the motif of the plowed earth penetrated to receive seed in the Straight Furrow variation (p. 58). In most patterns, among them Barn

Rolling Pin Star: quilt, appliquéd; red and white cotton; Stouffville, Ontario, ca. 1890. W. 178 cm, L. 181 cm (70, 71 in.). A fascinating pattern filled with movement. [P.C.]

Raising, Light and Dark, and Saw Log, the lights and darks are arranged to form large diamonds or diamonds within diamonds (p. 66); this repetition and symbolic doubling add to the potency of the motif.

There are several other variations of the Log Cabin pattern: Fence Rail, Zig-Zag, Seven Steps to the Courthouse, Pineapple or Windmill Blades, and Chevron. Although these strong, handsome quilts took much care and planning, they were never considered genteel enough to be used on guest beds or marriage beds.

Over the years, as conditions improved and life became easier, women continued to use quilts to express their feelings, but when more civilized conditions prevailed, women again became more discreet about revealing themselves and symbols became more obscure.

As the nineteenth century progressed, symbols as designs continued to be used, but fewer people were aware of their original meanings, since the older women who believed in spirits and in good-luck tokens had died. Once education became universal, young people began to scorn the knowledge passed on to them by their parents and grandparents, and a great cultural heritage was forgotten. A woman in 1900 could read and write, but she had lost a great deal of the folk knowledge that her mother had possessed.

In the early years in Canada, the limitations of the fabric available for making quilts forced improvisations. Unaccustomed ways were devised to fit the limited scraps of cloth into quilts of any kind. In most communities in the first years of settlement, it is unlikely that there were pattern books, but most older women knew how to design a few simple patterns by the old-fashioned method of folding and cutting shapes of cloth. Possibly some women had brought with them paper guides, sometimes cut from old letters or newspapers, to indicate the shapes and sizes of commonly used patterns. Patterns were shared. When a new quilt was shown, the visitor routinely asked for a copy of the pattern. It was a sincere form of flattery, and the maker of the original quilt would be disappointed, even insulted, if no one requested the pattern. These paper guides, sometimes with the original pattern name scribbled on them, were considered precious and saved throughout the years.

Although many quilt pattern names have significant meanings, some are simply called after popular expressions and games in vogue at the

Peony: quilt, appliquéd; cotton; red and buff (possibly faded green) on white background; Prince Edward County, Ontario, 3rd quarter 19th century. W. 155 cm, L. 204 cm (61, 80 in.). This quilt was made for a bed that could be seen from one side only, probably a slip bedroom off the parlor. [C.C.F.C.S.]

✿

Pattern Blocks Quilt: some pieced, some appliquéd; made by Elizabeth Fennel Van Alstine, Napanee, Ontario, ca. 1885, using a block saved from each quilt she sewed in her lifetime. W. 190 cm, L. 198 cm (75, 78 in.). Some quilt makers kept pattern blocks for reference. [P.C.]

✪

time the quilts were first made; others are whimsical and indicate a gentle sense of humor: Duck's Foot in the Mud, Toad in the Puddle, Drunkard's Path, Buzzard's Roost, Hole in the Barn Door, Johnny Round the Corner, Rolling Pin Star (p. 68), Eternal Triangle. Hole in the Barn Door, called after a familiar image in farmyards, has several unrelated names—Churn Dash, Picture Frame, Pig's Poke, and Fisherman's Reel, among others. Some names were changed at the whim of the quilt maker, and others had alternative names that were used if the original name was inappropriate. For example, Drunkard's Path was called Rob Peter to Pay Paul when made as a crib quilt, and Wandering Foot was called Johnny Round the Corner when used on a young boy's bed.

By the third quarter of the nineteenth century, pattern books began to find their way even into rural areas, and quilt patterns were printed in newspapers. *The Family Herald and Weekly Star*, published in Canada, usually printed a quilt pattern. Pattern books were still not plentiful and were passed around to be shared in communities, much as paper patterns had been. A quilt maker in Frontenac County, Ontario, told me:

> I remember there was a quilt pattern book we all used—a dandy, big, thick one with all kinds of patterns in it. We used to pass it around from house to house, and all of us took our patterns from it. I don't think any of us knew whose book it was after a while, and when we wanted to make a new quilt, we had to ask around to find out who had it now.

Most, perhaps all, of these pattern books originated in the United States, which resulted eventually in a certain uniformity of design in the New World. While symbols of procreation and fertility still appeared, marriage quilts were more concerned with sentimental love as the century wore on. Still, even in the first half of the twentieth century, people continued to be superstitious to a degree that is difficult for us to find believable today. This credulity was a legacy of the days when people actively believed in the constant presence of spirits. I can attest to the fact that some women living in 1940 did believe that the name of a bedcover could indeed influence the character of an impressionable young person who slept beneath it, and some women, perhaps immodestly, deliberately put an error in a quilt they admired because only God can make a perfect thing.

By the twentieth century, people had almost forgotten the original meanings of the designs they used on their bedcovers. At one time hearts were sewn only on cradle quilts and marriage quilts, but today one sees even experienced quilters using the heart motif on quilts designed for middle-aged married women. The original symbol is now just part of a pattern. As appliquéd flower and tree patterns became naturalistic rather than stylized, the symbolic significance of the early patterns was lost.

Nevertheless, the quilts women made continued to reflect their moods. In some cases a general contentment, or even a joyous outlook, is revealed in a quilt, while others show a deep unhappiness and discontent with the fate life has handed out to them. Victorian women considered it unseemly to expose their innermost feelings, and the making of quilts sometimes provided a medium through which they could express their emotions. My great-aunt used restrained patterns in her quilts, perhaps to avoid revealing the frustrations she must have experienced as a Presbyterian spinster who spent almost her entire life first looking after her ailing parents, then keeping house for two unmarried brothers. And no one of us will ever know for sure if the quilting designs she used on her bridal quilts were intended to be pumpkin seeds or simplified lovers' knots.

Despite the general use of pattern books, quilts with individuality continued to be made. Even simple, everyday patterns are magically transformed under the hand of an artist skilled in color with a gift for design. The type of set used makes a decided difference in the finished quilt. When blocks are sewn edge to edge, the various colors of the pattern blocks almost touch, creating a different picture from when the colors are separated with alternate blocks or striped sets. Borders are usually reserved for good quilts and can be highly decorative. There are times when they actually detract from the drama of the all-over picture created by a quilt. For example, a wide border on a Log Cabin quilt can reduce the powerful impact of the all-over image. Some quilt makers designed their quilts for specific beds. When a bed was placed in the corner of the slip room or small bedroom off the parlor, our thrifty and practical ancestors often made a border for only the side of the quilt that could be seen from the doorway (p. 69). It makes sense. Waste not, want not.

Experienced quilt makers usually kept for reference a finished block of every quilt they made and liked. This ensured that the pattern would not be lost. Sometimes when an aging woman was approaching the end of her career as a quilt maker, she assembled a quilt using the various blocks she had been saving. One such quilt (p. 70), which I bought at an auction sale at the Van Alstine house in Napanee, Ontario, is composed of pattern blocks of quilts made by Elizabeth Fennel Van Alstine, grandmother of the former owner. The quilt is worn, since Elizabeth Van Alstine was said to have used it on her bed during her last years so that she could look at it and remember her favorite quilts.

From the same household came a memory quilt apparently made for a bride who was marrying into the Van Alstine family. Individual signed and dated blocks were made by the bride, her mother, and various members of the Van Alstine clan. Looking at it, one can visualize a pleasant afternoon quilting party in 1871, with the sun shining on the snowbanks outside the modest house where the women of the family were gathered to meet and honor the bride-to-be and her mother.

There have always been a relatively small number of quilters who designed their own patterns. Pioneer women who made woolen quilts, often of homespun cloth, did this, partly from necessity and partly because it suited their independent natures. These pioneer quilts will be discussed in the next chapter.

A refreshing New World embroidered quilt was made by a young woman of Irish descent who lived on a farm near Fallowfield in Carleton County, Ontario, early in the nineteenth century (p. 39). It is of particular interest because family tradition tells us that she designed this bedcover because of her love for flowers, both those that grew wild and those of the garden. With her needle and wool, possibly handspun and home dyed, she has worked a nosegay into the central block and delicately colored portraits of thirty varieties of flowers into the other blocks of this lightly quilted linen bedcover. The quilt and its history have been handed down through three generations of her family; the last owners were her great-granddaughters, Teena and Ida Davidson of Ottawa, Ontario.

Pictorial or story quilts made in the middle and last half of the nineteenth century were not common, but occasionally a woman decided to paint a picture of her own designing. In pictorial quilts, the appliqué method is generally used, since the individual designs can be made and then stitched on the base to create a picture or a series of pictures embellished with embroidery.

Indian Hunt: quilt, appliquéd; cotton; multicolored on a white background; made by Lidia Petch Park and her sister in Oxford County, Ontario, ca. 1840. W. 167 cm, L. 197 cm (66, 78 in.). The quilt depicts a lively pioneer scene, with Indians on horseback hunting in the woods near a house with a picket fence, flower beds, and grape arbor. Birds, flowers, trees, and running dogs abound. The Indians, birds, flowers, even the finials on the fence posts and doorknobs, are stuffed. Details, such as the deer's antlers, the Indian headdresses, and the spots on the dogs, are embroidered. Lovely running-vine border. The women who made this quilt were fabric artists who would allow no one to see their work of art until it was completely finished. [P.C.]

✡

Diamond Rings: quilt, pieced; silks, assorted colors on black background; Dundas County, Ontario, last quarter 19th century. The daughter of the maker remembers her mother sent to Boston, Mass., for remnants advertised in the paper. Shimmery material gives the illusion of cut diamonds. Picot edging all around. [P.C.]

✧

ABOVE : *Windmill: quilt, pieced; glazed cotton; deep pink on dark blue; made by Mrs. Ferguson, Beachburg, Ontario, 1st quarter 20th century. W. 182 cm, L. 190 cm (72, 75 in.). The four large blocks making up this quilt are unusual, their appearance almost unrelated to the function of a bedcover; however, the result is dramatic. [C.C.F.C.S.]*

✧

RIGHT : *Memory Quilt: appliquéd; cottons; yellow, red, green on white background; one of a pair made by Margaret McGuire, Cornwall, Ontario, 1976. W. 155 cm, L. 223 cm (61, 88 in.). The maker of the quilt has appliquéd scenes dear to her heart: memories of her children, the cottage, the swing, the familiar birds, the cat, a little girl with her teddy bear. Pictorial quilts became popular about this time. [P.C.]*

✧

ABOVE : *Rideau Canal/Four Seasons: quilt, appliquéd; cotton, polycotton; designed by Carol Lee Riley; made by Storrington Retirees Association, Storrington County, Ontario, 1982. W. 215 cm, L. 213 cm (99, 84 in.). The design of the quilt depicts a history and a map of the Rideau Canal combined with a representation of the four seasons. Agnes Etherington Art Centre, Queen's University. Gift of the Storrington Retirees Association, with the assistance of Clifford and Currie Mahoney, 1984.*

✧

RIGHT : *The Bath Centennial Quilt: embroidered, appliquéd, pictorial; quilting: sculptural; cotton and polycotton; designed by Jessie Demaine; made by Associate Loyalist Quilters, Bath, Ontario, 1984; co-ordinated by Doris Waddell. W. 218 cm, L. 177 cm (86, 70 in.). Agnes Etherington Art Centre, Queen's University. Gift of the Associate Loyalist Quilters, assisted by Empire Life Insurance Company, Gibbard Furniture Shops Ltd., and Strathcona Paper Company.*

✧

A beautiful and unique pictorial quilt (p. 74) was made by Lidia Petch Park and her sister in Oxford County, Ontario, about 1840. Details of the lively appliquéd figures—native Indians on horses hunting deer and what may be a dream house (the women lived in a log cabin)— have charming touches of embroidery. This remarkable quilt was made as a work of art by the two sisters, who took great personal satisfaction in creative quilt making. They would allow no one to peek at the bed-cover until it was entirely finished.

A woman from Dundela, Ontario, ordered the silk material for her Diamond Rings quilt (p. 75) from a company in Boston, Massachusetts, that advertised remnants for sale. Probably this fascinating, shimmery quilt was intended for display as a parlor or spare-bed throw, since it would be unlikely to survive a washing. Certain quilts composed of four large pattern blocks, such as the Windmill pattern (p. 76) made in Renfrew County, Ontario, give the impression they, too, were designed as rather startling but effective pictures.

In the second half of the twentieth century, quilts that reflect the lifestyle of the quilt maker became fashionable. The maker of the Memory Quilt (p. 77) placed on each block a scene dear to her heart and the hearts of her children: familiar birds, the cottage, the swing, the family cat, and a tiny girl with her teddy bear. The charming quilt Rideau Canal/Four Seasons (p. 78), which depicts scenes of long ago, was made by a group of retired women who enjoyed the work so much they went right ahead and made a second one. A group of quilters in Bath, Ontario, made the attractive and important Bath Centennial Quilt (p. 79), depicting in each block the image of a historic building in the town. Many modern quilts must be looked on as pictures rather than bedcovers.

There is a school of modern quilt makers who create artworks using fabric and needle instead of canvas, paints, and brushes. Their handsome works could be considered a separate art form, but they, too, use two layers of cloth, sometimes with a filling layer between. Many of their quilts are made in unwashable fabrics of great beauty. These art quilts are meant to hang on walls, whereas most traditional quilts were meant to be used on beds. Most modern quilts, however, even those of a more traditional nature, are no longer intended as bedcovers to keep one warm but, like the "good" quilt of yesterday, are show quilts, planned to adorn a bed during daylight hours. Many of these new-style quilts are strikingly beautiful, and although usually abstract, some are intended to be allegorical.

Three examples of the fabric art of Ann Bird, which is known and acclaimed internationally, appear in this book: Northern Lights V (p. 86), Clear Cut, 1994 (p. 87), and Caribou Run, 1995 (p. 87). All three are expressions of Ann Bird's concern and love for the northern areas of Canada.

Canadian women of the nineteenth century lived in a world in which the seasons and the cycles of life dominated their lives. They inherited an ancient stock of folk knowledge, including the belief in spirits and demons. The symbols they carefully placed on their quilts were often the same as those placed on everyday objects: the furniture, cupboard and house doors, barns and implements in common use. Reminders of the times when people actively believed in the spirit world can still be seen throughout the countryside. A carved wooden pineapple (p. 82), the symbol of hospitality, can still be seen above a gable window of an old house in Renfrew County, Ontario. The same design can be found on the Pineapple quilt (p. 83), which was probably made for use on a guest bed. A few years ago, barns in Mennonite country, west of Toronto, Ontario, frequently displayed painted diamonds and sunlike images to encourage fertility, and hex signs to frighten away evil spirits. The Sunflower quilt top (p. 85) was made in the same area and displays many of the same symbols. The sunflower is usually considered symbolic of the male, and a plowed field (the striped set), in which the seed is planted, represents the female. The elaborate border has a fascinating array of vines with flowering hearts displaying the open hand of friendship, bushes in urns containing tulips, sheaves of wheat, and other flowers. There are also hex symbols to ward off evil and sunlike symbols to ensure fertility.

Large H–L (Holy Lord) hinges (p. 84) still remain on the door of an empty barn in Lanark County, Ontario. In an early quilt of brilliant red and black woolen cloth (p. 84), a woman in northern Lennox and Addington County, Ontario, has repeatedly pieced the letters H–L, standing for Holy Lord, presumably to protect the person sleeping beneath it. In Glengarry County, Ontario, a pair of garage doors, originally used as barn doors, reveal painted diamond fertility symbols. These probably had more meaning when the doors were on the barn, and knowing the courting habits of young people in that county, I question the wisdom of placing fertility symbols on a building that houses any car!

Pineapple: wooden carving on roof of old house, near Pembroke, Ontario, early 19th century. The pineapple was a symbol of hospitality, which appeared in carvings on old inns, sometimes on newel posts and fireplace surrounds. This house, no longer lived in, is situated between Highway 17 and the Ottawa River. It was possibly an old inn.

✡

Pineapple: quilt, appliquéd and pieced; cotton; Woodville, Ontario, 4th quarter 19th century. W. 167 cm, L. 177 cm (66, 70 in.). Elaborate quilts with pineapple patterns were sometimes made for guest beds.

[P.C.]

✿

These symbols and the beliefs that inspired them were the property of the whole family, understood and appreciated by all. If the lavish care that women took in making their quilts is a measure of their devotion to their families, the use of protective and emotional symbols in their designs is equally proof of their concern that their family should prosper, the children grow strong, and the marriages remain passionate. The images are beautiful, but they are also indicative of a knowledge that has disappeared.

ABOVE LEFT: *H–L Hinge: old iron hinge on barn door in Lanark County, Ontario. Such hinges were placed on barns doors and inside houses on room and cupboard doors to invoke the protection of the deity.*

✿

ABOVE RIGHT: *Quilt: pieced, handwoven of homespun wool; vividly colored orangey-red and black; Lennox and Addington County, Ontario, 2nd quarter 19th century. W. 162 cm, L. 205 cm (64, 81 in.). The H and L undoubtedly stand for Holy Lord, and are intended to protect the sleeping person.* [C.C.F.C.S.]

✿

Sunflower: quilt top, pieced; cotton with appliquéd border; Niagara Peninsula, Ontario, 3rd quarter 19th century. W. 212 cm, L. 212 cm (83, 83 in.). The sunflower symbolizes the male, and the plowed field (indicated by the striped set) the female. The border has a magnificent array of vines, urns, hex symbols, tulips, hearts, and sheaves of wheat. Notice the heart with the open hand in it, a commonly recognized symbol of friendship. The other symbols are intended to ward off evil and ensure fertility.

[C.C.F.C.S.]

✿

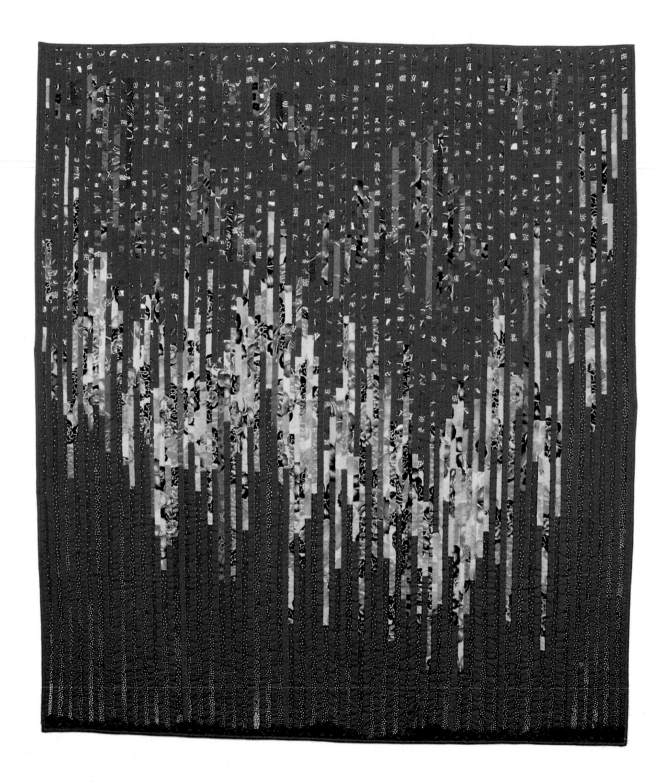

Northern Lights V: cotton; machine-quilted with metallic thread; by Ann Bird, Ottawa, Ontario, 1993. W. 132 cm, L. 147 cm (52, 58 in.). One of an ongoing series depicting the Northern Lights, so familiar in the Canadian skies.

✦

Clear Cut: cotton; machine reverse-appliquéd; machine-quilted; by Ann Bird, Ottawa, Ontario, 1994. W. 61 cm, L. 41 cm (24, 16 in.). Protest statement about the ugly bleakness of a logged horizon in northern Ontario and nature's endurance in putting forth new growth.

✧

Caribou Run: procion dyed cotton, cotton print; by Ann Bird, Ottawa, Ontario, 1995. W. 152.5 cm, L. 114.5 cm (60, 45 in.). A statement of concern about the danger to the ancient migratory traditions of the caribou herd in the North caused by human expansion and development.

✧

CHAPTER 5

Quilts of the Pioneers

At long last we are preparing to leave forever...as soon as possible we shall set foot on our travels to a new land of promise...We expect the journey to be long and hard, and cannot tell how many weeks we will be on the road...I leave this beautiful Mohawk valley and the lands I had hoped we should always hold...Our grandparents little thought when they sought this new land after the risings of Prince Charlie that a flitting would be our fate, but we must follow the flag wherever it takes us...

—From a letter by Nancy Jean Cameron, May 12, 1785

COLD AND LONELY SETTLERS LIVING IN ISOLATED log cabins in the virgin bush made our first Canadian quilts out of necessity. And that was about all they had with which to make quilts. Scraps of cloth from clothing too worn to hold together and threadbare blankets too thin for warmth were cobbled together and stuffed with feathers, dried grasses, milkweed silk, the down from bulrushes, sometimes even dried leaves that turned to powder before spring. Nothing tangible is left of those first desperate attempts to provide warmth, only stories passed down through the generations.

Two main groups arrived in Canada in the late eighteenth century: those who came in sailing ships from the Old World, mainly the British Isles; and those who came by foot from the British colony to the south, which is now the United States.

Scores of families from Scotland and Ireland were being driven from farms they had worked for generations by landowners who now wanted to raise sheep. These dispossessed farmers, with no way to make a living, were forced to leave forever the friendly villages of their homelands in

OPPOSITE PAGE:
Diamond and Square: quilt, pieced; handspun, handwoven wool; Leeds County, Ontario, second quarter 19th century. W. 152 cm, L. 195 cm (60, 77 in.). This was a common format in early wool quilts found throughout the eastern counties of Ontario. The diamond is a widely recognized symbol of fertility. This example is particularly powerful.
[C.C.F.C.S.]

✡

Variable Stars: quilt, pieced; 12 eight-point stars; handwoven woolen cloth, some manufactured; vivid colors; Enterprise area, Ontario, third quarter 19th century. W. 157 cm, L. 193 cm (62, 76 in.). A strikingly handsome quilt, both top and back.
[C.C.F.C.S.]
✳

search of fresh beginnings in the new country. With them on the immigrant ships they brought bedding to use during their journeys, but there was not enough space to bring extra bulky items such as quilts, which might be needed in the future.

About the same time, the English colony in America was rebelling against England. A large group of Scots, who had come to that land seeking freedom after the English had defeated the Scottish monarchy, now refused to fight England and were forced to migrate to Canada. With them came groups of people originally from Germany and Holland who would not participate in the American Revolution because their parents, victims of religious persecution in their home countries, had taken an oath of allegiance to the English king when they settled in the New World.

Many of them, martyrs of their overactive consciences, were on the move again. These early refugees from the south, first called Loyalists (later United Empire Loyalists), traveled on foot along the Indian trails through the bush, some with carts drawn by horses or oxen to carry food and household goods over the rough terrain. They, too, were able to bring with them only as much bedding as they needed for the trip, but unlike the new immigrants off the ships, they had already learned to adapt their traditional ways of making bedding to conditions in the harsh New World.

Most spent the first winter in army barracks, and when they moved out to their allotted land in the spring, they faced an untouched wilderness of vast, impenetrable underbrush and giant trees whose interlocking branches towered above their heads. The only roads were Indian trails and rivers. Their first houses were crudely made log cabins that sat in lonely solitude in small clearings in the dense bush. Both groups of settlers were aware that another terribly cold winter would be coming and somehow more bedding had to be acquired. These were resolute people, and, having survived months of living in the squalid holds of tossing sailing ships and walking endless miles through virgin bush, they no longer had any choice but to make what they could of their adversities. It was sink or swim.

The government supplied a minimum amount of bedding, but it was not nearly enough. Although immigrants had been forewarned, the first ones to arrive were ill-prepared for the harsh conditions. It was difficult to anticipate winters so severe that sometimes people asleep in bed actually froze to death. One of the many urgent tasks facing the bewildered and harassed new settlers was to procure warm bedding for their families.

Once in a long while, an old quilt, a rugged survivor of those times, turns up in an original homestead, where it has been cherished over the years as a memento of the early days. One quilt I have seen recently is said to have made the long trek from the Mohawk Valley with the Loyalists. This unique quilt was made by descendants of German immigrants who had settled in the Mohawk Valley some fifty years earlier.

Early pictures show immigrants from overseas burdened with huge bundles, and tucked in them one would expect to find some items brought over for sentimental reasons, such as a cherished family counterpane considered too good for everyday use. Similar mementos might also be found under the baggage on the ox carts.

It is, however, unlikely that any fragile bedcovers, no matter how precious, survived the urgent need for warm bedcovers in the first winters of the cold New World. When garments too worn to be used as clothing were carefully ripped apart to make quilts, even the thread was saved and reused. The practice of reusing cloth continued well into the twentieth century. Canadians did not easily forget the lesson of Waste Not, Want Not that was learned early in a pioneer country.

As late as 1887 Anna Leveridge, who with her seven children immigrated in 1883 to the northern part of Hastings County, Ontario, wrote to her mother in England:

> I have been, and am still busy at quilt making. Blankets are still so dear in this country that we have to make quilts to keep warm. I take care of all pieces of cloth out of old clothes and stitch them on the machine, line them and quilt them together, and they make warm, heavy bed coverings. Some of the quilts in this country are very pretty, pieces not much bigger than your finger all joined in patterns.[12]

Although some fabric could be obtained at backwoods stores, it was expensive and money was in short supply. In order to protect the English textile industry, manufactured American cotton fabrics were not allowed into Canada, although it is likely a certain amount of cloth made its way illegally across the border, since most Loyalist families had relatives who had remained in the States. Thread, too, was expensive and difficult to obtain. Fabrics were so scarce that badly worn quilts were used as fillings in the next generation of quilts. Remnants of early quilts indicate that quilt makers preferred to work designs into even the crudest of bedcovers. Pioneer women liked the order of well-defined forms and cut each scrap into a rectangle. It was not until the "crazy quilts" of the late nineteenth century became a fad that irregularly shaped pieces were sewn together to make tops.

Settlers could not make their own cloth until land was cleared to pasture sheep and grow flax. Clearing virgin forest took time, and even after the land was usable imported sheep often died from the cold or were destroyed by wild animals.

When a family finally had wool from its sheep and linen thread from home-grown flax, the women prepared the yarns and wove them into cloth for clothing or bedding. People who had no loom took their laboriously prepared yarns to the local home weaver, who did weaving for pay or, more commonly, for barter. The entire process involved much hard work for the family, but good warm cloth was essential in a pioneer community.

Although some of the quilts were, by necessity, crudely made, the designs used in these first bedcovers were bold and powerful. Rugged and unfriendly though the land appeared to be, the settlers, especially those from the old countries, were proud to be landowners at last. For generations, settlers such as the Scottish immigrants had worked land that they did not own. Now that they were landowners they exulted in their freedom, despite the hardships. The vivid colors and extravagant designs of the bedcovers reveal the pride and joy they felt in their new life. The brilliant quilts, with their unashamed large patterns, were flags of victory as they waved on the clotheslines.

When planning early quilts, busy pioneer women had no time or thought for subtle symbols such as peacocks whose flesh did not decay, butterflies who were resurrected, or flowering bushes that promised a fruitful life. Among the huge trees in the realm of raw nature, the primitive beliefs of their Old World ancestors in the spirits of trees and rocks and lakes seemed more significant. The spirit world was very close in this primeval wilderness, and the teachings of Christianity, although not forgotten or ignored, formed only a thin veneer over the ancient Druid beliefs. While people could not afford to give up the bulwark of the newer Christian religion, they dared not risk losing the sanctions of the old ways.

There was lavish use of symbols, but those appearing on bedcovers were simple and direct. People wanted to have children. This was a matter of prime importance. All members of the family knew that children were essential to help with the work, to inherit the new lands, and to build a network of relatives in the new country to provide help and ensure mutual protection. There was almost no privacy in crowded log cabins. Girls had to assist their mothers during childbirth, and in busy households young girls took on much of the care of the infants. All too often infants died, and the whole family knew how important it was to replace the lost ones.

Pioneer women were realistic. They could not afford to be prudish or whimsical. The symbols they placed on bedcovers were overtly sexual,

✡

involved with reproduction and showing concern for the day-to-day safety of their families. Here in the backwoods women felt it was their sole responsibility to protect their families from the dreaded spirits that might be roving in this untamed wilderness. While some of these unknown spirits might be good, others were undoubtedly evil. It was essential that the good ones be placated and the demons be frightened away. Anyone who has stood in a virgin forest knows the feeling of awe, amounting to terror, in the presence of the unleashed elements of nature.

The most commonly used design was the diamond, the widely recognized symbol of fertility. The female imagery represented by the diamond shape is obvious, and it appears over and over again on quilts made for everyday use (p. 88). A square within the diamond doubles the magic. A woman of German descent in Frontenac County told me her mother and grandmother always made striped quilts, which they quilted with "pure wool," and always quilted "an elongated circle in the center and smaller ones around the edges." This was probably a variation of the diamond image. Large stars were used frequently as patterns, and most stars were made by sewing together the diamond shapes (p. 90).

Although homemade cloth can be used in the natural colors of sheeps' wool, early quilt makers went to the additional work of dyeing their cloth brilliant reds and blues, bright oranges and soft yellows. Some of these colors could be produced by making dyes from native plants, but other dyes, such as red, had to be bought at the store. Log cabins were dark even in the daytime, and the only sources of light were homemade candles and the flames on the hearth. The brilliantly colored bedcovers were therefore both useful and exciting.

In her book *Patchwork*,[13] Averil Colby states there is evidence that homespun woolens were made into rough patchwork quilts in Scotland from the middle of the eighteenth century, although very little is known of them now. At this time the first Scottish people were already immigrating to the United States and, to a lesser

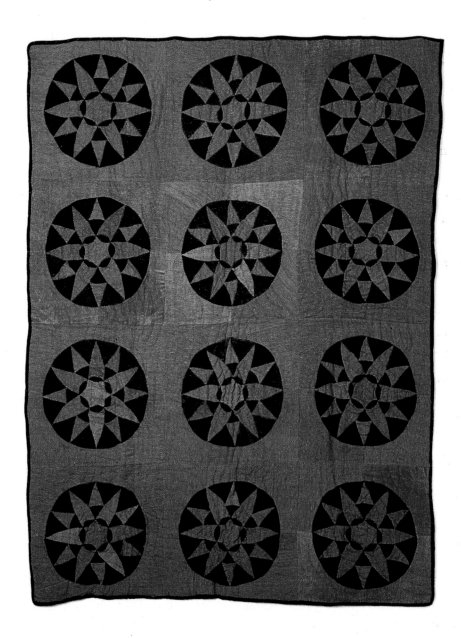

Harvest Sun: quilt, pieced; handwoven cloth of homespun wool with cotton weft; beautiful shade of rust or red and black; Scugog Island, Ontario, 3rd quarter 19th century. W. 172 cm, L. 217 cm (68, 85 in.). [S.S.M.]

✿

extent, Lower Canada. By the latter part of the century they were coming directly to Upper Canada. It is probable they brought the homespun tradition to Ontario, and here it flourished. There are many examples of homespun quilts still to be found in Ontario today. Many of these were made at a fairly late date, although early ones are still around, despite the ravages of time, wear, and neglect. These homespun quilts are most often found in homes inhabited by Scottish people, and were made there (p. 94).

Immigrants who came from the same districts in the homeland tended to settle in clusters in the new land. The women had been accustomed to making the traditional quilts of their home countries, and each distinct ethnic group had its own traditions, resulting in distinctive bedding patterns in the different districts. Right from the start, however, it was necessary to modify these traditions to suit the conditions of a new land, and in the course of time there was an gradual infusion of new ideas from other groups when they began to mingle and exchange ideas.

For these reasons, these early woolen quilts reflect the diverse racial origins of the settlers, rather than revealing the influence of any particular region in Canada. For example, early quilts made anywhere by people of Scottish origin have certain common characteristics, although those in any one district are influenced, as well, by conditions in that particular area. In Glengarry, for instance, which borders Quebec, both Scottish and French women had the same practical approach to quilt making. They rarely lost sight of the fact that a quilt was made to keep a body warm as well as to look decorative. Women of German origin who immigrated in the latter half of the nineteenth century continued to make wholecloth quilts, as did the women of their homeland. I have seen two wholecloth quilts in Renfrew County, Ontario, that came over with the original owners from Germany in the third quarter of the nineteenth century. The wool in these quilts was softer, finer and less springy than Canadian wool. The entire surfaces of the European bedcovers were intricately quilted in elaborate spirals or whorled patterns. Many hours had gone into the making of these designs. They were probably made by women who had more leisure time for needlework than did the pioneer women of Renfrew County. While most Renfrew County woolen quilts are also closely quilted, often with homespun yarn, the patterns are simpler. Some are tufted or tied. The two quilts made in Germany were all-over brown in color, but the Canadian quilts have vividly colored striped designs woven into woolen cloth. Renfrew County was settled late, and some women of German descent were spinning and weaving cloth until the first quarter of the twentieth century.

Wholecloth quilts were made and used to a lesser extent in other areas, especially in the eastern counties of Ontario and in areas west of Toronto, which were settled both by Scots and Germans. Bedcovers woven in brightly colored crosswise stripes were used in Quebec, but the stripes were random in width, rather than woven into definite patterns, as were those of Renfrew County, and those I have seen are unbacked and unquilted.

In the late eighteenth and early nineteenth centuries, large numbers of German Loyalists from the United States settled in the counties in Upper Canada bordering on the St. Lawrence River. In Stormont County, for example, their descendants continued to weave during the entire nineteenth century. Yet I have seen no distinctly German quilts in those districts, although there are many excellent handwoven coverlets and blankets. Either the settlers did not make wholecloth woolen quilts anymore, or, because the area was settled at a very early date and these were people who prided themselves in keeping up-to-date, they did not hold on to their early quilts through the years.

Many Canadian women are traditionalists who like the old ways. There are quilts of homespun cloth made in Ontario as late as the third quarter of the nineteenth century, some in quite elaborate patterns, like the lovely Harvest Sun (p. 95), which even makes use of appliqué. In these later quilts, the quilting is finely done, even though homespun yarn, which must have been difficult to draw through the layers of wool cloth and filling, is sometimes used. In earlier examples, quilting was kept to a minimum because thread was scarce and there was little time to spend at the work.

The heavy woolen quilts we inherited from our ancestors have not been well used, but fortunately they can stand much abuse. They are so heavy that people stopped using them on beds as soon as houses were easier to heat and fabrics for lighter quilts became available.

In our family, my mother and grandmother put the old woolen quilts on the floor for the babies to crawl on. My father folded another one behind the stove to make a bed for his old hound. They were relegated to the cottage, where their warmth was welcome in the cold, damp dawns, and they made ideal rugs to sit on in the tall grass. When I moved into a rural area north of Kingston, Ontario, I was told that all the old heavy quilts had been sent "up North to the missions" a few years earlier.

Like most quilts, they are not all equally attractive, but all are interesting and some are superb. They are also our most original expressions in creative quilts and reflect the indomitable spirits of our hardy ancestors who settled these lands.

General Instructions, or Helpful Hints

1. If you are using templates from any book or magazine, check them for accuracy before cutting out your fabric. This can be done easily with a ruler for squares, triangles, etc.

For more complicated patterns, I use paper shapes and put them together like a jigsaw puzzle.

2. When templates are shown with a seam allowance, and you are going to use them that way, there are a few guidelines to ensure accuracy:

First, your 0.6 cm (¼ in.) marking tool should be checked against the template to ensure that it measures the same.

Second, after marking your seam allowance on your fabric, check that the measurement inside the pencil line matches that of the template.

3. Placing your pieces "right" sides together, you should first match and pin your seam allowance junction points, and then place pins along the pencil lines matching both sides. It is important that your stitches be on the lines of both fabrics.

4. Squares and triangles are usually easier to deal with later if they are sewn from one raw edge to the other. Hexagons and diamonds normally need to have 0.6 cm (¼ in.) left open at both ends for pivoting, and are therefore sewn from junction point to junction point and not sewn across the seam allowances.

5. When pressing (and I mean pressing, not ironing!), do NOT open the seams as you would in dress making (this will weaken them)—rather press them to one side, together.

6. When sewing strips of pieces together, the seams will come together more neatly if you press them in alternate directions before sewing.

7. As far as possible, keep the lengthwise grain of the fabric pieces on the lengthwise grain. It helps with the finished appearance of your piece.

8. Thread is wound onto the spool in one direction, and if you change that, it tangles! It is best, therefore, to make a knot on the freshly cut end before threading your needle from the other side.

9. Pieces are sewn together with a small but simple running stitch, anchored at the beginning and end of the seam to ensure security.

10. The blind stitch used in appliqué is a hemming stitch done underneath and on the edge of the pieces, and should be smallish, not tiny, and invisible from the front.

11. Quilting should always be done on a frame or hoop, since it keeps the back from moving, and ensures straight stitches front and back.

12. A "pivot stitch" is used to turn corners when inserting a third piece into an inward angle made by sewing two diamonds or hexagons together.

   The stitch is best defined as a simple running stitch from the outside junction point of "A" to the center junction point of "B", and then from the inside junction point of "B" to the outside junction point of "C".

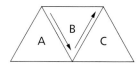

Three Tulips in a Pot

This naturalistic pattern was popular during the 1920s and 1930s, when quilters wanted patterns that were a fair representation of the subject they portrayed. The actual quilt is pictured on p. 38.

Finished size: W. 173 cm, L. 195 cm (68, 77 in.).
✿

Fabric requirements

All fabric is 115 cm (45 in.) wide.

Background fabric	4.5 m	(5 yd.)
Green lattice	3.0 m	(3.3 yd.)
Pots 2 shades	0.7 m each	(0.8 yd.)
Stems and leaves	1.0 m	(1.1 yd.)
	(stems cut on bias)	
Flowers:		
peach 2 shades	0.7 m each	(0.8 yd.)
mauve 2 shades	0.7 m each	(0.8 yd.)
Binding	0.8 m	(0.9 yd.)
Backing	5.0 m	(5.5 yd.)

Regular sewing supplies, including:

- washable marking pencil for use on the *right* side of your fabric;
- sewing thread to match background fabric;
- sewing thread to match the strongest colour of your flowers;
- basting thread;
- pins, needles, scissors, etc.

General Instructions

1. Please make the templates exact. Use plastic or cardboard.

2. Cut out ten squares for appliqué: 42 cm (16½ in.) for each block.

3. From the green fabric for the stems and leaves, cut about 8 m (26 ft.) of 2 cm (¾ in.)-wide flat bias (not folded). Use the rest of the same green fabric for the leaves.

4. Draw around the outside edges of the templates, on the *right* side of the fabric, using washable pencil.

5. Cut out the pieces, adding at least an extra 0.6 cm (¼ in.) all around the perimeter of the pieces.

6. Clip curves only if necessary. On all pieces, sharp turns must be clipped right up to the pencil line (see below).

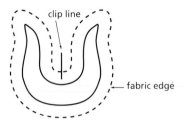

7. To make sharp points, fold the seam allowance under the tip. Then fold the seam allowances on either side of the point.

8. Baste back the extra fabric with contrasting colored thread. This is most easily done from the front of the piece, and close to the edge.

9. Trim away extra fabric from the back, leaving only slightly less than 0.6 cm (¼ in.) of seam allowance.

10. Placement on the background fabric must be traced onto *right* side of the background square. (If diagram is not given, use diagonal or straight folds as a guide.)

The order in which you place and appliqué your pieces is usually self-explanatory. The stems are usually first. If a flower has a smaller flower and a center on it, you can separately appliqué these onto the larger flower first, and then place the complete flower on the background fabric.

11. For circles, it is sometimes helpful to stitch around the edges within the seam allowance first, in a running stitch, and then place the circle template in the center. Draw up the thread around the template, and tie a knot. Then press the enclosed template/fabric with an iron and damp cloth. Let dry, then remove the template.

12. After layering all pieces in proper position on the background square, pin, then baste them in place. Basting is most effective if done close to the edge of each piece, not just generally holding it down.

13. Using a blind stitch, attach the pieces to the background.

14. Referring to the photograph of this quilt, you will notice large triangles of background fabric around the edges. Nine of these are made by cutting five 43 cm (17 in.) squares in half diagonally; and the other two are made of one 33 cm (13 in.) square cut diagonally.

15. Lattice fabric is cut in lengthwise strips, 6.3 cm (2½ in.) wide; and then sub-divided as follows:

A	16	42 × 6.3 cm	(16½ × 2½ in.)
B	1	88 × 6.3 cm	(34½ × 2½ in.)
C	1	184 × 6.3 cm	(72½ × 2½ in.)
D	1	235 × 6.3 cm	(92½ × 2½ in.)
E	1	143.5 × 6.3 cm	(56½ × 2½ in.)
F	2	179 × 6.3 cm	(70½ × 2½ in.)
G	2	209.5 × 6.3 cm	(82½ × 2½ in.)

16. Assemble the blocks and triangles in diagonal strips, with lattice between, as in the diagram. Finish with the top and bottom borders, then the sides.

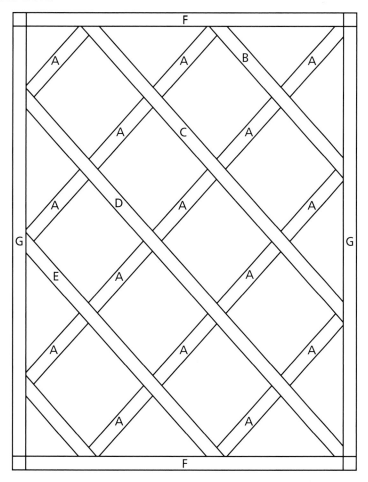

←—1"—→

This template is not full size. One square equals 2.5 cm (1 in.). Add a 0.6 cm (¼ in.) seam allowance around the perimeter of each piece.

✺

Sampler Quilt

The quilt pictured on page 2 is called a "Sampler" because each of the thirty blocks is of a different construction. This enables the quilter to make samples of these whilst practicing new techniques of assembly.

We have included a Quilt Plan for this purpose, and to start you off we are offering instructions for four of the original blocks for you to try. You may choose to make a whole quilt of one of these blocks (e.g., Pilgrim's Progress), or add more 30 cm (12 in.) blocks of your own choosing, to follow the tradition as the original quilter did.

Happy quilting!

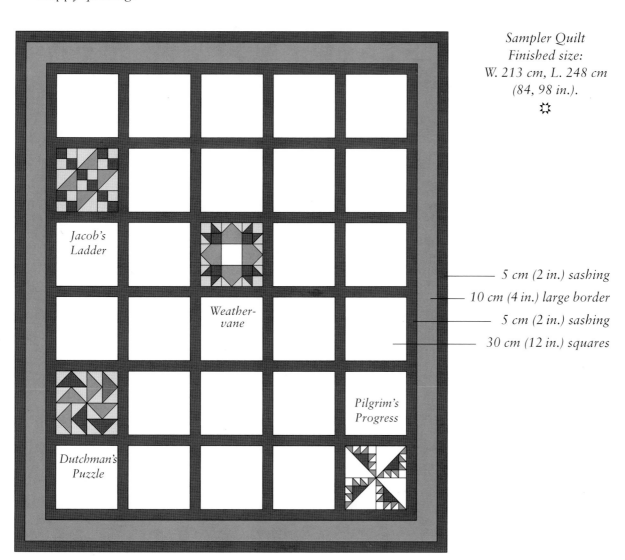

Sampler Quilt
Finished size:
W. 213 cm, L. 248 cm
(84, 98 in.).
✡

Jacob's Ladder

Weather-vane

Pilgrim's Progress

Dutchman's Puzzle

— 5 cm (2 in.) sashing
— 10 cm (4 in.) large border
— 5 cm (2 in.) sashing
— 30 cm (12 in.) squares

Fabric Requirements for the Sampler Quilt

All fabric is 115 cm (45 in.) wide.

For blocks:	scraps or 1.0 m (1.1 yd.) assorted mediums and	
	1.0 m (1.1 yd.) assorted darks	
Background for all blocks:	2.0 m (2.2 yd.) assorted lights	
Sashing and outside border:	2.7 m	(3.0 yd.)
Larger border:	2.6 m	(2.8 yd.)
Binding:	0.7 m	(0.8 yd.)

Pilgrim's Progress

Instructions

1. Using Template B (see p.107), cut out twenty-four strong and sixteen light triangles. Pin at the seam allowance, junction points, and sew across the longer (bias) side (using 0.6 cm [¼ in.] seam), joining sixteen sets, to form squares.

2. Now join those squares into eight sets of two, as follows.

4 each A

4 each B

3. To each of your A sets, add one of the leftover triangles from Step 1.

and join these to the straight-grain side of the strong pieces cut from Template D.

4. To each of your B sets, add one of the leftover triangles and a light-colored square (Template C).

5. Now join these to the other side of the assembled piece from Step 3. Sew this piece to your large light triangle (Template A).

6. Set four segments together to form a pinwheel in the centre. (Read the General Instructions page for detailed hints to improve your accuracy.)

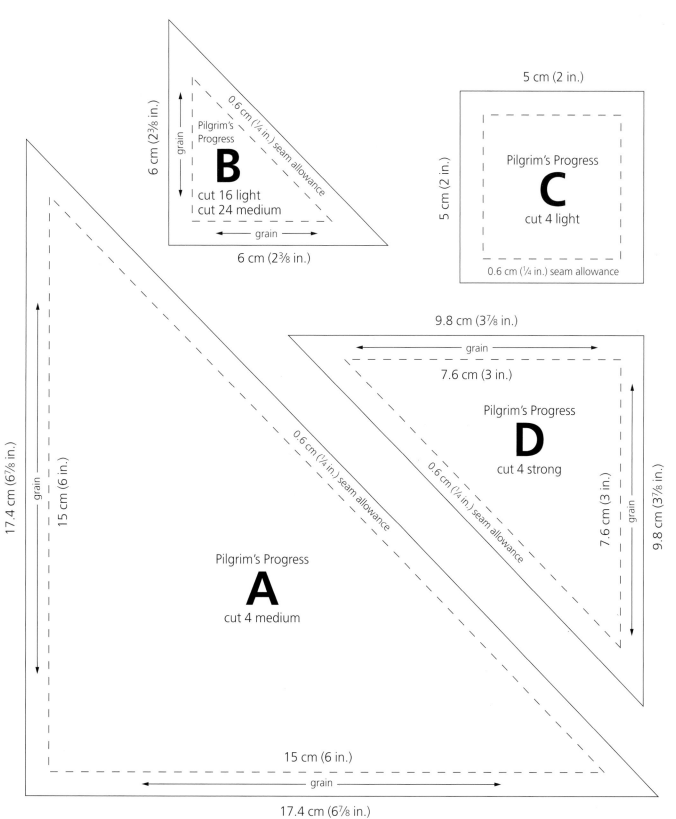

Dutchman's Puzzle

Instructions

1. Cut sixteen light pieces using template A and eight strong pieces using Template B.

2. Sew these together as eight "Flying Geese" units.

3. Piece these together in four sets of two.

4. Join sets to form two rows.

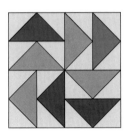

5. Join rows to form block.

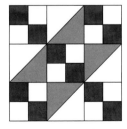

Jacob's Ladder

Instructions

1. Cut ten light print and ten strong 6.3 cm (2½ in.) squares using Template D, and sew them together to form five "Four Patch" squares.

2. Using Template C, cut out four strong and four light triangles and sew them together to form four squares.

3. Make three rows of three squares each, alternating as in diagram.

4. After pinning junction points to ensure they meet, sew rows together to form block.

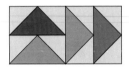

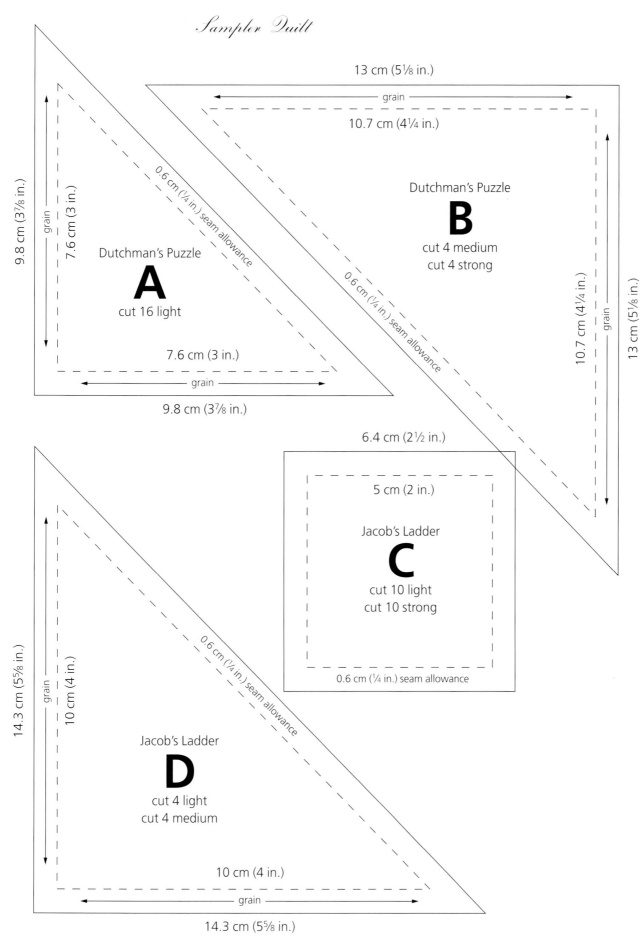

Dutchman's Puzzle

A

cut 16 light

9.8 cm (3⅞ in.)

grain

7.6 cm (3 in.)

0.6 cm (¼ in.) seam allowance

7.6 cm (3 in.)

grain

9.8 cm (3⅞ in.)

13 cm (5⅛ in.)

grain

10.7 cm (4¼ in.)

Dutchman's Puzzle

B

cut 4 medium
cut 4 strong

0.6 cm (¼ in.) seam allowance

10.7 cm (4¼ in.)

grain

13 cm (5⅛ in.)

6.4 cm (2½ in.)

5 cm (2 in.)

Jacob's Ladder

C

cut 10 light
cut 10 strong

0.6 cm (¼ in.) seam allowance

14.3 cm (5⅝ in.)

grain

10 cm (4 in.)

0.6 cm (¼ in.) seam allowance

Jacob's Ladder

D

cut 4 light
cut 4 medium

10 cm (4 in.)

grain

14.3 cm (5⅝ in.)

Weathervane

Instructions

1. Using Template A, cut out eight strong and sixteen light triangles. Pinning at the seam allowance junction and sewing across the bias side (using 0.6 cm [¼ in.] seam), join eight sets to form squares.

2. Using Template B, cut out four light squares and join to four Step 1 squares, as follows –

Then cut out strong dark squares and join to Step 1 squares as follows –

3. Join sets made in Steps 1 and 2 to form four squares.

4. Using Template C, cut out four from medium fabric and sew remaining light triangles from Step 1 to form four units –

5. Cut out one dark 11.4 cm (4½ in.) square (Template D) and join your pieces into rows as in diagram. Sew rows to form block.

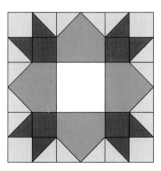

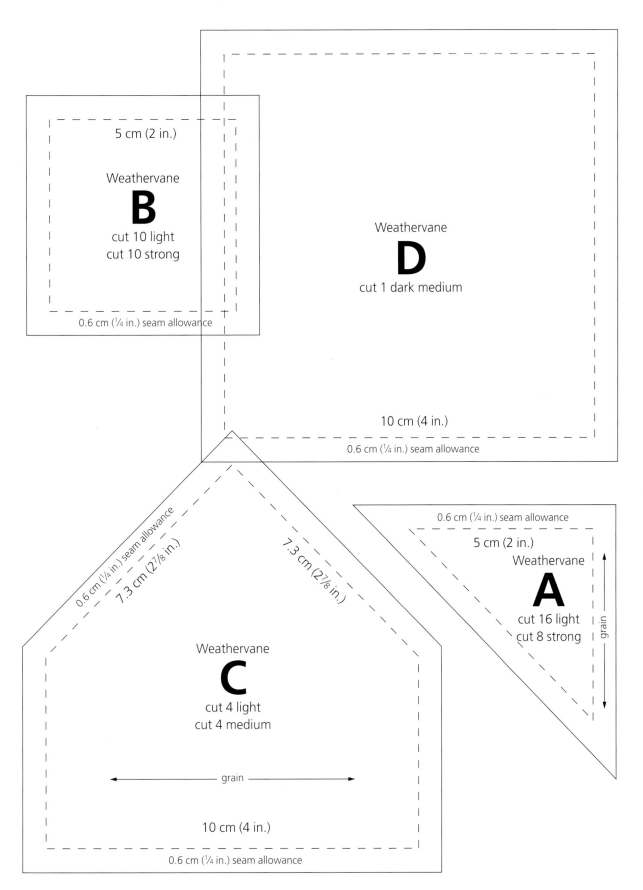

5 cm (2 in.)

Weathervane

B

cut 10 light
cut 10 strong

0.6 cm (¼ in.) seam allowance

Weathervane

D

cut 1 dark medium

10 cm (4 in.)

0.6 cm (¼ in.) seam allowance

0.6 cm (¼ in.) seam allowance

7.3 cm (2⅞ in.)

7.3 cm (2⅞ in.)

Weathervane

C

cut 4 light
cut 4 medium

grain

10 cm (4 in.)

0.6 cm (¼ in.) seam allowance

0.6 cm (¼ in.) seam allowance

5 cm (2 in.)

Weathervane

A

cut 16 light
cut 8 strong

grain

Birds in Flight

*This is a more accurate rendering of the quilt pictured on page 30.
The measurements given here will make a 137 cm (54 in.)-square wall
quilt to show off an embroidered piece in the center, or you can make
a 61 cm (24 in.) pieced or appliquéd block to frame as follows.*

*Finished size:
W. 137 cm, L. 137 cm
(54, 54 in.)*

Fabric Requirements

All fabric is 115 cm (45 in.) wide.
For blocks: mixed scraps or 1 m (39 in.) each light, medium, and
strong dark or bright colors.

Inside border:	0.4 m	(0.4 yd.)
Outside border:	0.4 m	(0.4 yd.)
Binding:	0.5 m	(0.5 yd.)

Instructions

1. Take your inner border fabric, cut two strips, 9 × 62 cm (3½ × 24½ in.). Match the center and ends of the border with the center and ends of the quilt. Pin. Sew one of these strips to the top of your 61 cm (24 in.) center block and another to the bottom.

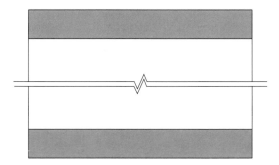

2. Next, cut four 9 cm (3½ in.) squares (Template B) as cornerstones and sew one onto each end of the remaining strips. Then, matching seam allowances, join those to the sides of your center piece.

3. Using Template A, cut out forty strong bright triangles and forty medium or light triangles. Sew these into 9 cm (3½ in.) squares.

Then join together four sets of ten squares each. One of these triangle strips is sewn to the top of the assembled square, another to the bottom.

4. Now cut out four 9 cm (3½ in.) squares (Template B) for corner-stones, and sew one onto each end of the remaining triangle strips. Matching seam allowances, join those to the sides.

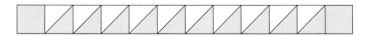

5. From your second border fabric (could be the same as the first) cut four strips, 9 × 93 cm (3½ × 36½ in.). Add four more cornerstones (Template B) from another fabric or the same one as before to the ends of two strips. Join these, top and bottom and sides, as in previous instructions.

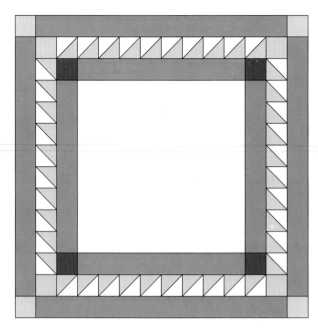

6. Using Template C, cut 80 dark and 64 light squares. Stitch 32 rows with a light center and 16 rows with a dark center. Assemble blocks as illustrated.

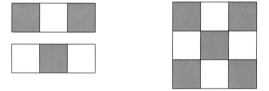

7. Cut out sixteen Template D squares in contrasting tones from the "Nine Patch", so as not to blend in.

8. Alternating the "Nine Patch" and Template D squares, make four strips as per finished diagram and sew onto assembled top.

9. Quilt and bind.

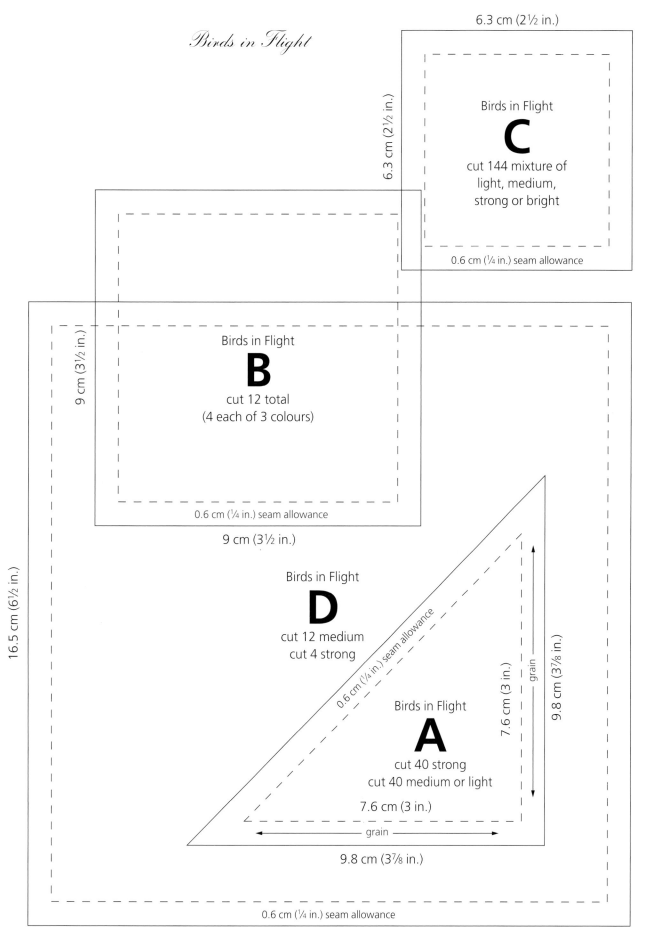

6.3 cm (2½ in.)

6.3 cm (2½ in.)

Birds in Flight

C

cut 144 mixture of
light, medium,
strong or bright

0.6 cm (¼ in.) seam allowance

9 cm (3½ in.)

Birds in Flight

B

cut 12 total
(4 each of 3 colours)

0.6 cm (¼ in.) seam allowance

9 cm (3½ in.)

16.5 cm (6½ in.)

Birds in Flight

D

cut 12 medium
cut 4 strong

0.6 cm (¼ in.) seam allowance

grain

7.6 cm (3 in.)

9.8 cm (3⅞ in.)

Birds in Flight

A

cut 40 strong
cut 40 medium or light

7.6 cm (3 in.)

grain

9.8 cm (3⅞ in.)

0.6 cm (¼ in.) seam allowance

16.5 cm (6½ in.)

Endnotes

CHAPTER 1
Fruit of Her Hands

1. Information about this early inventory can be found in *The Early Furniture of French Canada* by Jean Palardy (Toronto: Macmillan of Canada, 1963), p. 365.

2. W.L. Stone, *Letters of Brunswick and Hessian Officers during the American Revolution* (Albany, N.Y.: 1881), pp. 13, 16–20.

3. D.M. Brockster, *Diagrams of Quilt Sofa and Pin Cushion Patterns* (St. Louis, Mo.: Ladies Art Company, 1898), pp. 1–10.

4. Ladies Art Company, *Catalogue of Quilts and Quilting* (St. Louis, Mo.: Ladies Art Company, 1898), pp. 1, 23, 24.

5. Ladies Art Company, *Quilt Patterns Patchwork and Appliqué* (St. Louis, Mo.: Ladies Art Company, 1928), p. i.

6. Information from a Red Cross wartime directive.

CHAPTER 2
The Quilting Bee and the Marriage Bed

7. [Michael Scherck], *Pen Pictures of Early Pioneer Life in Upper Canada* (Toronto: William Briggs, 1905), p. 194.

8. Job 38:7.

CHAPTER 4
Quilt Patterns, Their Meanings and Origins

9. Song of Solomon 2:1–3, 9–13.

10. Genesis 2:9.

11. John 15:5.

CHAPTER 5
Quilts of the Pioneers

12. Louis Tivey, *Your Loving Anna: Letters from the Ontario Frontier* (Toronto: University of Toronto Press, 1972), p. 95.

13. Averil Colby, *Patchwork* (London: B.T. Batsford, 1958), p. 28.

Bibliography

ARMSTRONG, NANCY CAMERON, ed. *Patchwords*. Vols. 1, 2. White Rock, B.C.: Canadian Quilt Study Group, 1992, 1994.

ARSENAULT, GEORGES. *Acadian Folk Art of Prince Edward Island*. Catalogue. Prince Edward Island Heritage Foundation, 1982.

BACON, LENICE INGRAM. *American Patchwork Quilts*. New York: William Morrow and Company, Inc., New York, 1973.

BARSS, PETER. *Older Ways: Traditional Nova Scotian Craftsmen*. Toronto: Van Nostrand Reinhold, 1980.

BISHOP, ROBERT, and PATRICIA COBLENTZ. *New Discoveries In American Quilts*. New York: E.P. Dutton and Company, Inc., 1975.

BURLEIGH, HERBERT C., ed. *Samuel Sherwood's Account Book 1785–1810*. Kingston: Dr. H.C. Burleigh, 1975.

BURNHAM, DOROTHY K. *Pieced Quilts of Ontario*. Toronto: Royal Ontario Museum, 1975.

———. *The Comfortable Arts: Traditional Spinning and Weaving in Canada*. Ottawa: National Gallery of Canada, 1981.

———. *Unlike the Lilies: Doukhobor Textile Traditions in Canada*. Toronto: Royal Ontario Museum, 1986.

BURNHAM, HAROLD B., and DOROTHY K. BURNHAM. *Keep Me Warm One Night*. Toronto: University of Toronto Press, 1972.

CAMERON, NANCY JEAN. Letter, dated May 12, 1785, from Nancy Jean Cameron in Braedalbian, New York, to her cousin Margaret McPherson in Blair Athol, Perthshire, Scotland. A photostat of a copy of this letter is in the possession of the author.

COLBY, AVERIL. *Patchwork Quilts*. London: B.T. Batsford, 1965. Reprinted 1988.

———. *Patchwork*. London: B.T. Batsford, 1971.

———. *Quilting*. New York: Charles Scribner's Sons, 1971.

CONROY, MARY. *Canada's Quilts*. Toronto: Griffin Press, 1976.

CRUICKSHANK, E. A. "Captain John Waldon Meyers, Loyalist Pioneer." *Ontario Historical Society*, Vol. XXXI (1936).

FIELD, RICHARD HENNING. *Spirit of Nova Scotia: Traditional Decorative Folk Art 1780–1930*. Catalogue. Halifax: Art Gallery of Nova Scotia, 1985.

FINLEY, RUTH E. *Old Patchwork Quilts and the Women Who Made Them*. Newton Centre, Massachusetts: Charles T. Brandford Company, 1970.

HADERS, PHYLLIS. *Sunshine and Shadow: The Amish and Their Quilts*. New York: Universe Books, 1976.

HALL, CARRIE A., and ROSE KRETSINGER. *The Romance of the Patchwork Quilt in America*. Caldwell, Idaho: Caxton Printers, 1935.

HOLSTEIN, JONATHAN. *Artists' Quilts: Quilts by Ten Contemporary Artists in Collaboration with Ludy Strauss*. Catalogue. Published in association with Harold I. Huttas, 1981.

———. *The Pieced Quilt, A North American Tradition*. Toronto: McClelland and Stewart, 1973.

HOLSTEIN, JONATHAN, and JOHN FINLEY. *Kentucky Quilts 1800–1900*. The Kentucky Quilt Project. New York: Pantheon Books, 1982.

KING, ELIZABETH. *Quilting*. New York: Leisure League of America, 1934.

LADIES ART COMPANY. *Catalogue of Quilts and Quilting*. St. Louis, Missouri: Ladies Art Company, 1898.

———. *Diagrams of Quilt Sofa and Pin Cushion Patterns*. St. Louis, Missouri: Ladies Art Company, 1898.

———. *Quilt Patterns Patchwork and Appliqué*. St. Louis, Missouri: Ladies Art Company, 1928.

LEE-WHITING, BRENDA. *Harvest of Stones, The German Settlement in Renfrew County*. Toronto: University of Toronto Press, 1985.

McKENDRY, BLAKE. *Folk Art: Primitive and Naïve Art in Canada*. Toronto: Methuen, 1983.

McKENDRY, RUTH. *Quilts and Other Bed Coverings in the Canadian Tradition*. 1979. Reprint. Toronto: Key Porter, 1985.

———. *The Heritage Quilt Collection*. Catalogue. Kingston: Agnes Etherington Art Centre, 1992.

MONTGOMERY, FLORENCE M. *Printed Textiles, English and American Cottons and Linens, 1700–1850*. New York: Viking Press, 1970.

O'BRIEN, MERN. *Early Nova Scotia Quilts and Coverlets*. Catalogue. Halifax: Dalhousie Art Gallery, 1981.

ORLOFSKY, PATSY, and MYRON ORLOFSKY. *Quilts in America*. New York: McGraw-Hill, 1974.

PALARDY, JEAN. *The Early Furniture of French Canada*. Toronto: Macmillan Company of Canada, 1963.

PATTERSON, NANCY-LOU. "Log Cabin Quilts." *Canadian Collector* (Nov./Dec. 1977): 40–44.

ROBSON, SCOTT, and SHARON MACDONALD. *Old Nova Scotian Quilts*. Halifax: Co-published by Nova Scotia Museum and Nimbus Publishing Limited, 1995.

SAFFORD, CARLETON L., and ROBERT BISHOP. *America's Quilts and Coverlets*. New York: E.P. Dutton and Company, 1972.

[SCHERCK, MICHAEL.] *Pen Pictures of Early Pioneer Life in Upper Canada, by a "Canuck"*. Toronto: William Briggs, 1905.

STRICKLAND, SAMUEL. *Twenty-seven Years in Canada West*. 2 vols. 1853. Reprint. Edmonton: M.G. Hurtig, 1969.

SURM, LAURIE. *The Joy of Quilting*. Toronto: Viking Canada, 1984.

TIVEY, LOUIS. *Your Loving Anna: Letters from the Ontario Frontier*. Toronto: University of Toronto Press, 1972.

WALKER, MARILYN L. *Ontario's Heritage Quilts*. Toronto: Stoddart, 1992.

Index

Page numbers in italics refer to illustra-
tions.

Agnes Etherington Art Centre, Queen's
    University, illustrations of quilts in
    collection: 6, 31, 34, 39, 41, *55*, 78,
    79
Apple Orchard, 29, *34*
Associate Loyalist Quilters, 78

Barn Raising, 68
Bath Centennial Quilt, 79, 80
Bath, Ontario, 78, 80
Beachburg, Ontario, 76
Beaver, *8*
Bee, quilting, 22, 24
Bird, Ann, 81, 86, 87
Birds in a Tree, *16*, 62
Birds in Flight, *42*, *61*, 62, *65*
Birds in Paradise, 62
Birds in the Air, 62
Blocks, 12
Borders, 55, 72, 81
Bridal quilts: *see* Quilts, marriage
Buzzard's Roost, 71

Campbell, Jessie, 7
Canada Goose, Waterlilies, and Cattails,
    64
Canada Lily, 62
Canadian Centre for Folk Culture
    Studies, illustrations of quilts in col-
    lection: 10, 16, 18, 20, 21, 23, 26, 27,
    30, 31, 33, 37, 40, 46, 58, 61, 66, 69,
    76, 84, 85, 88, 90
Canadian Quilt Study Group, 22
Caribou Run, 81, *87*
Carleton County, Ontario, 65, 73
Cherry Tree and Birds, 63
Chimney Swallows, 62
Chimney Sweep, 19, *20*
Churn Dash, 71
Cleaning quilts, 56–57
Clear Cut, 81, *87*
Cloth: *see* Fabric
Colby, Averil, 94
Colonial Girl, 29
Color, 24, 28, 29, 32, 36, 45, 49, 54, 56,
    72, 94
    and design and construction, 57, 72
Cornwall, Ontario, 76
County fairs, 53
Crozier, Amelia, 51

Davidson, Teena and Ida, 73

Delectable Mountains, 19, *21*, *23*, *25*
Demaine, Jessie, 78
Diamond and Square Quilt, *88*
Diamond Rings, *75*, 80
Dodge, Betsey, 46
Double Hearts, *31*
Double Wedding Ring, 29
Double Wild Goose Chase and Star, *17*,
    19
Dresden Plate, 29
Drunkard's Path, 71
Duck's Foot in the Mud, 71
Dundas County, Ontario, 74
Dundela, Ontario, 80
Durham County, Ontario, 45, 46
Dyes, 24, 94

Eastern Star, 52
Emotions expressed in quilts, 7, 49, 72
Enterprise, Ontario, 90
Eternal Triangle, 71

Fabric, types used, 15, 28, 45, 92, 94, 97
    limitations of available, 69
Fallowfield Quilt, 35, *39*
Fallowfield, Ontario, 39, 73
Family Herald and Weekly Star, The, 71
Fence Rail, 68
Ferguson, Mrs., 76
Fisherman's Reel, 19, 71
Fraser, Hatty, 28
French Star, 19
Friendship Aster, 29
Frontenac County, Ontario, 47, 71, 94
Full Blown Tulip, 35, *40*, 62

Garland, Jega Matilda, 43, 65, 67
Gatineau Point, Quebec, 38
Geometric Star, 15, *16*
German influence on quilt making, 96
German Loyalists, 97
Glenburnie, Ontario, 43, 67
Glengarry County, 15, 19, 81, 96
Glengarry, Ontario, 28
Goose Foot in the Mud, 62
Goose in the Pond, 62
Goose in the Window, 62
Grenville County, Ontario, 46

Harpin, Mme., 17
Harvest Sun, *95*, 97
Hastings County, Ontario, 92
Hole in the Barn Door, 19, 71
Hovering Hawks, *12*
Huntingdon, Quebec, 7

Huron County, Ontario, 94

Indian Hunt, *74*

Jack in the Pulpit, 29, *37*, 62
Johnny Round the Corner, 71

Kingston Heirloom Quilters, 41
Kingston, Ontario, 41, *55*, 56

Lanark County, Ontario, 40, 81, 84
Lansdowne, Ontario, 64
Laurier, Mrs. John, 38
Leeds County, Ontario, 11, 26, 65, 66, 89
Lemon Star, 19
Lennox and Addington County, Ontario,
    37, 81, 84
Leveridge, Anna, 92
Light and Dark, 68
Little Beech Tree, 63
Little Houses, *54*
Log Cabin, 67, 68, 72
Log Cabin, Barn Raising variant, *66*
Log Cabin, Straight Furrow, *58*
Loyalists, German, 97

Mary Morris Quilt, 26, *27*
McAndrew, Elizabeth Hannah, 18, 19,
    20, *21*, *23*, *25*
McGinn, Catherine, 30
McGregor, Annie, 16
McGuire, Margaret, 76
Memory Quilt, 73, 76, 80
Montreal, Quebec, 30
Morris, Mary, 24, 26, 27, 65
Mulligan, Frances, 24, 30, 65

Napanee, Ontario, 70, 73
Newboyne, Saskatchewan, 18, 19, 20,
    21, 23
Niagara Peninsula, Ontario, 85
Noon Day Lily, 62
North Carolina Lily, 62
Northern Lights V, 81, *86*

Old Brown Goose, 7, *18*, 19, 62
Old Fashioned Basket, *55*, 56
Old Rose of Sharon, 12, *14*
Orillia, Ontario, 34
Ottawa, Ontario, 73, 86, 87
Oxford County, Ontario, 74, 80

Park, Lidia Petch, 74, 80
Pattern Blocks Quilt, *70*
Pattern

books, 19, 52, 71, 72
commercial patterns, 19, 24–25, 29
designing, 69
designs, early, 93
exchanging, 24
inspiration, 59
names, 69–71
pictorial, 80
sharing, 69
Patterns
  Apple Orchard, 29, *34*
  Barn Raising, 68
  Bath Centennial Quilt, 79
  Beaver, *8*
  Birds in a Tree, *16*, 62
  Birds in Flight, *42, 61, 62, 65*
  Birds in Paradise, 62
  Birds in the Air, 62
  Buzzard's Roost, 71
  Canada Goose, Waterlilies, and
    Cattails, *64*
  Canada Lily, 62
  Caribou Run, 81, *87*
  Cherry Tree and Birds, 63
  Chevron, 68
  Chimney Swallows, 62
  Chimney Sweep, 19, *20*
  Churn Dash, 71
  Clear Cut, 81, *87*
  Colonial Girl, 29
  Delectable Mountains, 19, *21, 23, 25*
  Diamond and Square, *88*
  Diamond Rings, 75, 80
  Double Hearts, *31*
  Double Wedding Ring, 30
  Double Wild Goose Chase and Star,
    17, 19
  Dresden Plate, 29
  Drunkard's Path, 71
  Duck's Foot in the Mud, 71
  Eternal Triangle, 71
  Fallowfield Quilt, *39*
  Fence Rail, 68
  Fisherman's Reel, 19, 71
  Frances Mulligan Quilt, *30*
  French Star, 19
  Friendship Aster, 29
  Full Blown Tulip, 35, *40*, 62
  Geometric Star, 15, *16*
  Goose Foot in the Mud, 62
  Goose in the Pond, 62
  Goose in the Window, 62
  Harvest Sun, 95, 97
  Hole in the Barn Door, 19, 71
  Hovering Hawks, *12*
  Indian Hunt, *74*
  Jack in the Pulpit, 29, *37*, 62
  Johnny Round the Corner, 71
  Lemon Star, 19
  Light and Dark, 68
  Little Beech Tree, 63
  Little Houses, *54*
  Log Cabin, 67, 68, 72

Log Cabin, Barn Raising variant, 66
Log Cabin, Straight Furrow, *58*
Mary Morris Quilt, *26, 27*
Memory Quilt, 76, 80
Noon Day Lily, 62
North Carolina Lily, 62
Northern Lights V, 81, *86*
Old Brown Goose, 7, *18*, 19, 62
Old Fashioned Basket, *55* , *56*
Old Rose of Sharon, 12, *14*
Overall Bill, 29
Pattern Blocks Quilt, *70*
Peony, *69*
Picture Frame, 71
Pig's Poke, 71
Pine Tree, 63
Pineapple, 68, 81, *83*
Pumpkin Seed, 63
Rambler Rose, 29
Rideau Canal/Four Seasons, *78*, 80
Rob Peter to Pay Paul, 71
Rolling Pin Star, *68*, 71
Rose Cross, *14*
Rose of Sharon, 35, *40*, 63
Sampler Quilt, *41*
Saw Log, 68
Seven Steps to the Courthouse, 68
Star of Bethlehem, 45, *46*
Straight Furrow, 67
Sunbonnet Sue, 29
Sunflower, 81, *85*
Swallow in the Path, 62
Swallow's Flight, 62
Swallow's Nest, 62
Swallows in the Window, 62
Three Tulips in a Pot, 29, *38*
Toad in the Puddle, *37*, 71
Tree Everlasting, 63
Tree of Life, 63
Tree of Paradise, 29, *33*, 63
Tree of Temptation, 63
Tudor Rose, 63
Variable Stars, *90*
Velvet Sampler, *50*
Wandering Foot, 71
Whig's Defeat, *6*
Wild Geese Flying, 62
Wild Goose Chase, 62, *94*
Windmill Blades, 68
Windmill, 76, 80
Zig-Zag, 68
Pen Pictures of Early Pioneer Life in
  Upper Canada, 44
Peony, 69
Picton, Ontario, 53
Picture Frame, 71
Pig's Poke, 71
Pine Tree, 63
Pineapple Quilt, 81, *83*
Pineapple, 68
Portsmouth Village, Ontario, 61
Prince Edward County, Ontario, 33, 69
Pumpkin Seed, 63

Quilt patterns: *see* Patterns
Quilters of Princess Street United
  Church, 55
Quilting bee
  and marriage, 43–45, 48
  twentieth century, 47–48
  waining of, 46–47
Quilting groups, 22
  Associate Loyalist Quilters, 78
  Canadian Quilt Study Group, 22
  church, 29, 32, 35, 36, 47, 56
  Kingston Heirloom Quilters, 56
  Quilters of Princess Street United
    Church, 55
Quilting
  as aesthetic expression, 36
  as expression of emotion, 49, 72
  bee, 22, 24, 47
  before 1860, 12–15
  in British Columbia, 22
  and church groups, 29, 32, 35, 36, 47,
    56
  destruction of traditions, 32
  in eighteenth century, 15, 97
  influences on, 15
  in Maritimes, 19
  in nineteenth century, 15, 19, 22, 24,
    46–47, 52, 53, 59, 60, 62, 63, 64,
    67, 68, 71, 73, 81, 96, 97
  in Ontario, 15, 19, 22, 95
  in Quebec, 15
  and Second World War, 32
  symbols: *see* Symbols
  in twentieth century, 15, 19, 22, 28,
    32, 52, 53, 71, 72, 80, 96
  in the west, 19
Quilts
  appliquéd, 12, 28, 29, 57, 59, 62, 73,
    97
  as art, 80–81
  cleaning, 56–57
  comfort, 32
  construction of, 12, 45, 55, 67, 72, 89
  cradle, 72
  crazy, 28, *31*, 92
  crib, 71, 72
  everyday, 45, 57, 59
  German, 96, 97
  history in North America, 15, 89–97
  homespun, 95
  ideal, 55
  manufactured, 36
  marriage quilts, 24, 43–45, 48, 49,
    59, 63, 64, 65, 68, 71, 72
  ornamental, 28–29, 36, 53, 80–81
  patchwork, 12, 15, 94
  pictorial, 73, 80
  pieced, 12, 57, 59, 60, 62
  qualities of well-made, 55
  Scottish, 94, 96
  story, 73
  striped, 94

types of, 12
wholecloth, 12, *13*, 96, 97

Rambler Rose, 29
Renfrew County, Ontario, 13, 59, 80, 81, 96
Rideau Canal/Four Seasons, *78*, 80
Riley, Carol Lee, 78
Rob Peter to Pay Paul, 71
Rolling Pin Star, *68*, 71
Rose Cross, *14*
Rose of Sharon, 35, *40*, 63

Sampler Quilt, *41*
Saw Log, 68
Scottish influence on quilt making, 96
Scugog Island, 95
Scugog Shores Museum, 95
Set, 12
Seven Steps to the Courthouse, 68
Sharbot Lake, Ontario, 28, 31
Soulanges County, Quebec, 16
St. Ours, Quebec, 17
Star of Bethlehem, 45, *46*
Stormont County, Ontario, 97
Storrington County, Ontario, 78
Storrington Retirees Association, 78
Stouffville, Ontario, 68
Straight Furrow, 67
Sunbonnet Sue, 29
Sunflower Quilt, 81, *85*
Swallow in the Path, 62
Swallow's Flight, 62

Swallow's Nest, 62
Swallows in the Window, 62
Switzerville Road, Ontario, 51
Symbols, 11, 27, 28, 30, 59–60, 62–65, 67–69, 71–72, 81, 84, 93
  birds, 64
  bushes, 81
  butterflies, 64, 65, 67, 93
  diamonds, 60, 68, 81, 94
  fertility, 63, 71, 81, 94
  flowering branch, 67
  flowering bush, 63, 64, 67, 93
  flowering vines, 60
  flowers, 62, 65, 67, 72
  flying bird, 62, 67
  goose, 62
  hearts, 65, 81
  hex sign, 67, 81
  Holy Lord (H–L), 7, 81, *84*, *85*
  lily, 62
  lovers' knots, 60
  number three, 65
  oak leaf, 60
  peacocks, 65, 67, 93
  pineapple, 81, *82*
  plowed earth, 67, 81
  procreation, 71
  rose, 62–63, 67
  rosettes, 60
  running vine, 63, 65
  scalloped circle, 65
  scallops, 67
  sexual, 67, 93

stars, 60, 94
sun, 60, 81
swallow, 60, 62
tree, 63, 72
twisted ropes, 60
vines, 81
windmill blades, 60

Thousand Island Branch of Rebecca Lodge, 64
Three Tulips in a Pot, 29, *38*
Toad in the Puddle, *37*, 71
Torrance, Ada, 34
Tree Everlasting, 63
Tree of Life, 63
Tree of Paradise, 29, *33*, 63
Tree of Temptation, 63

United Empire Loyalists, 91

Van Alstine, Elizabeth Fennel, 19, 70, 73
Velvet Sampler, *51*, *55*

Wedding quilts: *see* Quilts, marriage
Whig's Defeat, 6
Wholecloth Quilt, *13*
Wild Geese Flying, 62
Wild Goose Chase, 62, *94*
Windmill, 80
Wood, Mary Ellen, 62
Woodville, Ontario, 83

Zig-Zag, 68